a SAVOR THE SOUTH® *cookbook*

Fruit

a SAVOR THE SOUTH® *cookbook*

Fruit

NANCIE McDERMOTT

The University of North Carolina Press CHAPEL HILL

Designed by Kimberly Bryant and set in Miller and
Calluna Sans types by Rebecca Evans.

The University of North Carolina Press has been a member
of the Green Press Initiative since 2003.

Cover photograph: © istockphoto.com / Kaan Ates

Library of Congress Cataloging-in-Publication Data
Names: McDermott, Nancie, author.
Title: Fruit / by Nancie McDermott.
Other titles: Savor the South cookbook.
Description: Chapel Hill : The University of
North Carolina Press, [2017] | Series: A savor the South
cookbook | Includes bibliographical references and index.
Identifiers: LCCN 2016043314| ISBN 9781469632513
(cloth : alk. paper) | ISBN 9781469632520 (ebook)
Subjects: LCSH: Cooking (Fruit) | Cooking, American—
Southern style. | LCGFT: Cookbooks.
Classification: LCC TX811 .M43 2017 | DDC 641.6/4—dc23
LC record available at https://lccn.loc.gov/2016043314

To my friend and mentor Nathalie Dupree,
whose bold, extraordinary work paves the way,
and whose wisdom, insight, generosity, and spirit
make the way deliciously rewarding and fun

Contents

SIDEBARS

a SAVOR THE SOUTH® cookbook

Fruit

Introduction

outhern fruits are an essential, beloved gift of the hot
sticky weather and fertile soil of the region. Gathered in
the wild, or cultivated with care, plucked from trees and
pulled off vines, they see us through the seasons. Sweet
summer berries, fragrant melons, and globe-shaped
autumn grapes distract us from the heat, quench our thirst, and
decorate our pantry shelves with rows of jam-filled jars. From
bluegrass to sea grass, from red clay fields to bayous, and from
the Carolina Low Country to the Great Smoky Mountains, sweet
southern fruits thrive all around us, heralding the passage of time
while offering simple, transient pleasures throughout the year.

Here in Piedmont North Carolina, you-pick-'em strawberry
farms beckon us each spring. Savvy farmers entice us with the
pleasures of harvesting their carefully tended berry patches, freed
from the chores of planting and weeding en route to strawberry
shortcake. Luscious, ripe blackberries mitigate the July sun's
glare, and scuppernongs and muscadines provide welcome shade
under backyard arbors as the grape vines leaf-out. Late-summer
figs remind us to make preserves so that fig cake can be part of
cold-weather celebrations. Persimmons ornamenting their spin-
dly branches each autumn invite us to make old-time persimmon
pudding—so easy, so good, and so emblematic of fall's pleasures.

From Maryland, Florida, and West Virginia down to New Or-
leans, Houston, and the Mississippi Delta, we have a long, sweet
tradition of feasting on a gracious plenty of southern fruits. We
gather them to enjoy in season, and take time to preserve them in
sweet and savory versions to see us through the year. This book
spotlights a dozen of the best-loved and particularly southern of
these fruits: blackberries, cantaloupes, damson plums, figs, mayhaws, muscadine and scuppernong grapes, pawpaws, peaches,
persimmons, quince, strawberries, and watermelon.

These dozen natural wonders vary in numerous ways. You'll find wild mayhaws and grapes and carefully tended peaches and figs. Some ripen in spring, while other signal the arrival of summer and fall. Some are delicious right off the tree or vine, while others are impossible to enjoy until they are cooked. Some grow all over the South, while some are particular to one region and barely known elsewhere. Each has its charms, inviting us to slow down a bit, to learn a little history, to do some preparation or cooking in order to fully enjoy its goodness.

Half of the fruits featured in this volume are native to the southern United States. These include blackberries, mayhaws, muscadines and scuppernongs, pawpaws, wild persimmons, and strawberries. Not only are all six still growing wild in the southern landscape, but nowadays, they are cultivated around the South as well. That means we can often find them without mounting an expedition, and in some cases, even grow them at home.

The other six fruits featured in this book found their way to the South from elsewhere. Though not native-born, these were adopted long ago, eagerly welcomed, and invited to make themselves at home. This group of now deeply rooted southern heirlooms include cantaloupes, damson plums, figs, peaches, quince, and watermelon.

Not all the delectable fruits that bless the South made it into this book. With a limited number of pages, I had to decide which ones to feature and which to omit. With more than two dozen candidates and space for half that number, I went with the quintessentially southern ones, a few of which are lesser known and underappreciated in comparison to their status in the past. While apples, pears, blueberries, raspberries, and nectarines have a proud place on the southern table, they are also widely known and appreciated outside the South. Honeydew melons, crabapples, sour cherries, and mulberries fit on the long list, too, but lack the iconic southern stature of blackberries, watermelons, and figs. I hope that the fruits presented here intrigue and please you, and that you will be inspired to research and celebrate them.

Until the last few decades, none of these traditional southern fruits needed our help to be seen, maintained, and loved. Today, with so much on our plates, literally and figuratively, the need is there. This book is an invitation to notice them, seek them out, share them, and enjoy them in the kitchen and at the table.

These twelve southern fruits are more than simply memorable and lovely. Each one illuminates the South's regional distinctions as well. For me, peaches signify the sand hills of South Carolina, where the plump, fuzzy, juicy harbingers of summer remain a roadside attraction for drivers en route from Piedmont North Carolina to the beach. Hand-lettered signs used to beckon us along the two-lane state roads. Nowadays enormous billboards expand on that tradition, bidding us to pull off the interstate and indulge in a bushel of peaches for pies, jams, or cobblers or for passing around to the folks back home.

Pawpaws reward hikers exploring the Blue Ridge and the Great Smoky Mountains, as well as in-the-know foragers in forested areas near Washington, D.C. Small, sweet, bug-and-bird-attracting figs grow in luscious abundance wherever it's hot, and especially in the coastal climates from the Carolina Low Country and the North Carolina Outer Banks down to Florida, and along the Gulf Coast over to Louisiana and Texas.

Southern fruits matter, both as mementoes of the gardening and gathering of culinary seasons past and as worthy edible treasures for the present and future South. With the twenty-first-century enthusiasm for do-it-yourself pursuits in the kitchen, and with chefs employing professional foragers to gather good things from the natural world, these southern treasures are on home and restaurant menus once again. This awareness is a gift, a precious one to which we must pay grateful and action-oriented attention. Let's seek them out and support farmers who grow them, foragers who find them, and cooks who serve them. Let's grow them at home, eat them, cook with them, put them up, and reclaim the old ways that nourished our ancestors. These fruits and many more indigenous and adopted plants and foods deserve our enthusiastic attention as cooks, eaters, and students determined to savor the South.

This book aims to celebrate southern fruits as a lovely and worthy aspect of our history. Let's preserve them in our memory and on our kitchen counters. How sweet would it be to make it so that the little ones coming along behind us will know and love the fruits of the South? Let's make sure these fruits grow in abundance so that we can share them with future generations, teaching them just how sweet, ripe, refreshing, colorful, and naturally fine the South can be.

Blackberries

I love blackberries for what they are—beautiful blue-black, bubbly, and juice-filled balls of sweet-tart goodness. I adore them plain, simmered in syrup, cooked to jam, or baked into cobblers and pies. I also love them for what they bring to mind: Picking wild blackberries with my grandmothe`r when I was around seven years old on a blistering-hot, sun-bleached North Carolina morning. Picture my sisters and me, seat-beltless and squirming on the hot vinyl–covered backseat of an enormous white Ford Galaxy. The windows have been rolled all the way down, every surface is hot to the touch. We roll along winding roads into the country, half an hour north of my grandparents' dairy farm, to a long straight stretch of two-lane road lined with ditches. The banks above the ditches are covered with wild blackberry canes, and we are there to fill buckets with enough blackberries for jam, jelly, and Grand-mother's blackberry rolls.

I remember heat, the hot wind when the car was moving, and the way the car tilted downward on the red-dirt shoulder toward the ditch. I remember watching out for thorns but no thoughts about snakes. None showed up, but the effects of thorns, mosquitoes, chiggers, and sunburn were my souvenirs. Focused entirely on blackberry rolls, I didn't mind these costs. Blackberry rolls were saucer-sized circles of pie dough, with a pile of blackberries in the center, sugar, butter, pinches of flour, and salt. I can see my grandmother gathering the piecrust edges together to make a plump dumpling, which she wedged into a big enameled-tin biscuit pan just a tad smaller than the oven rack on which it would rest. Once she'd filled the pan with plump berry packets, she showered them with sugar, dotted then with butter, sprinkled them with water, and positioned the pan in the middle of the oven. I still remember seeing the pan pulled from the oven in the sultry summer afternoon kitchen, gorgeously gooey with purple syrup bubbling up from inside the berry bundles.

The wild blackberries that southerners gather in the summer heat belong to the Rose family and the *Rubus* genus, closely related to raspberries and dewberries. These hardy perennial plants grow on tall vertical canes, covered with thorns and tenacious about populating vacant lots, woodlands, wastelands, and those steep banks along the interstates throughout the south. These irresistible treasures grow around the world, with no clear origin story and confusion about particular species. The Greeks and Romans put blackberries to medicinal use, and Native Americans were using them as food and medicine and in making twine and dyes long before European contact.

Blackberries thrive in England's hedgerows or brambles, the dense, vibrant thickets that serve as boundaries between properties in the English countryside. Blackberries share their brambles with *bullace* and sloes, two types of wild plums, as well as birds and small creatures in need of the protection they provide. In the twentieth century, horticulturists focused on cultivating thornless blackberries, quickly finding success in getting the general details right, although developing cultivars with good flavor took longer than getting rid of the thorns. Beloved in sweet pastry creations, blackberries were also the basis for wine and cordials in colonial times, with the latter often made with herbs and other ingredients believed to provide medicinal value.

Today we find cultivated blackberries in the supermarket, fresh and frozen, as well as at farmer's markets, produce stands, and pick-your-own farms. The wild ones are still out there, so if you hanker for a little outdoor foraging, check out those hillsides, woodsy edges of parking lots, and vacant lots in spring, when curving rods of thorny canes sporting pretty, white-petaled blossoms offer you an invitation to come find some blackberry gold once the summer heat is firing up those June and July days.

Blackberry Roly Poly

This rolled-up berry-filled spin on the cobbler concept was once as common as upside-down cake is today. Its popularity faded away, but what a worthy treat to bring back! Biscuit dough is rolled out into a thick sheet, spread with melted butter, studded with plump blackberries, and sprinkled with sugar. Then it's jelly-roll time, in which you roll the far edge toward you and form a plump, lumpy cylinder, which bakes until golden and surrounded by little rivers of syrup. You can slice it or simply scoop it out into bowls—either way, enjoy it with a simple blackberry sauce and a generous portion of vanilla ice cream or whipped cream.

FOR THE ROLY POLY

2 cups all-purpose flour

1 tablespoon sugar

1 tablespoon baking powder

1 teaspoon salt

4 tablespoons very cold butter

About $\frac{2}{3}$ cup milk

1 cup (2 sticks) butter, melted

2 cups blackberries, fresh or frozen

1 cup sugar

FOR THE BLACKBERRY SAUCE

1 cup blackberries, fresh or frozen

$\frac{1}{3}$ cup sugar

$\frac{1}{4}$ cup water

Heat the oven to 400°.

To make the roly poly, in a large bowl, combine the flour, the 1 tablespoon of sugar, the baking powder, and the salt. Chop the 4 tablespoons of butter into small bits, scatter them over the flour mixture, and toss well. Using a pastry blender, two knives, two forks, or your hands, cut the butter into the flour until you have a raggedy, lumpy mixture with pea-sized bits of butter still showing. Add the milk and use your hand or a big spoon to transform the dry mixture into a dough. Turn it out onto a floured counter or cutting board and knead gently until you have a nice soft dough, about 5 turns.

Set the dough on a floured sheet of parchment paper, large enough to line an 11 × 17-inch sheet pan. Roll it out into a rectangle about 10 × 12 inches and about ¼ inch thick, with the long edge facing you, parallel to the counter. Pour the melted butter over the center portion of the dough, and spread it out evenly, leaving a 1-inch border. Scatter the berries evenly over the buttered dough, leaving a 1-inch border all around the edges. Sprinkle the 1 cup of sugar evenly over the buttered dough and berries.

Reaching across the dough to the far edge, gently roll the long edge of the dough toward you, enclosing the sugared berry filling. Roll it as tightly as you can, using the parchment paper to help you manage the unwieldy shape. Stop rolling when the open edge is on the bottom, and let this be the center seam underneath the roll. Carefully transfer the roll on its parchment paper bed to the baking pan. Bake at 400°for 30 minutes, or until the roly poly is nicely browned and firm, and the doughy center of the roll is cooked through.

While the roly poly is baking, make the sauce. Combine the 1 cup of blackberries, the sugar, and the water in a medium saucepan and bring to a rolling boil over medium-high heat. Stir well and adjust the heat to let it boil gently. Using a potato masher or a large metal slotted spoon or a big fork, mash the berries to release their juice as they cook. Cook for 5 minutes, stirring and mashing occasionally, or until the berries have released their juice and have formed a lightly thickened sauce. To remove the seeds, press the berry mixture through a fine-mesh strainer over a bowl and scrape the rounded outside of the strainer to capture every drop of the rich, sweet berry sauce. Set aside until the roly poly is ready.

When the roly poly is ready, let it cool for at least 10 minutes. Slice and serve hot or warm, or at room temperature, with the sauce drizzled over each slice. Serve with ice cream or whipped cream on the side if you like.

Blackberry Fool

Fools are a classic English pudding: simple, satisfying and elegant. They date back to the seventeenth century, with two versions, one antique and the other more common today. Sweetened and stewed fruits define them, with a soft custard as the original foundation. Whipped cream was often folded into the custard along with the fruit. Modern fools are made with whipped cream only, making them a spur of the moment option requiring only cream, sugar, and a bowl full of ripe sweet fruit. Gooseberries are the quintessential fool, but raspberries and blackberries are also beloved, and offer stunningly beautiful color to enhance the pleasures of being "fooled." Add a teaspoon of lemon or lime zest if you'd like a brighter note, and consider making a parfait, holding out some of the jam to use in making pure berry layers in a tall glass serving dish.

MAKES 4–6 SERVINGS

2½ cups blackberries, divided

½ cup sugar

¼ teaspoon salt

2 cups heavy cream

¼ cup confectioners' sugar

1 teaspoon pure vanilla extract

In a medium saucepan, combine 2 cups of the blackberries, the sugar, and the salt. Bring to a gentle boil over medium-high heat. Stir well to dissolve the sugar into the berries and help them release their juice. Adjust the heat to maintain a gentle boil and cook, stirring often and scraping the pan with a spatula, until you have a thick, glossy, lumpy, jammy sauce. Remove from the heat and let cool to room temperature. To cool it quickly, transfer it to another bowl and stir it often to release heat.

In a large bowl, beat the cream with an electric mixer at medium-high until it thickens and begins to hold its shape. Increase the speed to high and add the confectioner's sugar to the bowl. Beat, stopping to scrape the bowl often, until the cream has increased in volume and is very firm, but not dry.

When the berry sauce has cooled, add it to the bowl of whipped cream, folding it in gently using a spatula or a large spoon. You can mix it in completely, or leave some of the jam showing in ribbons of color and providing bursts of flavor. Spoon the fool into serving bowls, mounding it up handsomely for each serving. Garnish with remaining berries and chill until serving time. Serve cold.

Blackberry Slump

What a forlorn little name for a simply delightful and homey dessert! Also known as a grunt, this simple treat begins with ripe blackberries simmered with sugar and a little flour to make a thick, jammy berry compote. Then stir together a very soft biscuit dough and scoop it into walnut-sized dumplings, which you drop onto the sweet, bubbling berries and their juice. Simmered briefly, they puff up nicely into pleasing pillows of berry-kissed dough. Serve your blackberry slump warm, and consider adding a scoop of vanilla ice cream, a dollop of whipped cream, or a generous pour of cream, half-and-half, or evaporated milk.

MAKES 4–6 SERVINGS

FOR THE BLACKBERRIES
½ cup sugar
1 tablespoon all-purpose flour
½ teaspoon salt
3½ cups blackberries
½ cup water

FOR THE DUMPLINGS
1 cup all-purpose flour
1 tablespoon sugar
2 teaspoons baking powder
¼ teaspoon salt
2 tablespoons cold butter, cut into small pieces
¼ cup whole milk

To make the berry compote, combine the sugar, flour, and salt in a medium saucepan or a small Dutch oven. Stir with a fork to mix them well. Add the berries and water and stir gently. Place over medium-high heat and bring the berries to a gentle boil. Adjust the heat to maintain a lively simmer and stir well. Cook, stirring often, until the berries are surrounded by a thickened, shiny sauce, about 5 minutes. Remove from heat and cover to keep warm.

To make the dumplings, combine the flour, sugar, baking powder, and salt in a medium bowl, and stir with a fork to mix them well. Toss the butter into the flour mixture. Using your hands, press and squeeze the butter to incorporate it into the flour mixture, working it until you have a dry mixture with pea-sized lumps. Add the milk and stir well to make a very soft dough, like biscuit dough only more moist.

Return the berry compote to the stove and bring to a gentle boil over medium-high heat. Adjust the heat to maintain the boil. Using two teaspoons or a tablespoon, scoop up the dough and drop it onto the bubbling surface of the berry compote, making walnut-sized dumplings. When all the dumplings are in, reduce the heat to maintain a very gentle simmer and cover. Cook undisturbed for 15 minutes, or until the dumplings are dry and firm and cooked through. If you aren't sure they are done, remove and pull apart a large dumpling. Remove from the heat and serve hot or warm.

NOTE ✳ While a slump is best served as soon as it is ready, you can cool it and keep refrigerated for one day. To serve, reheat gently, adding about ¼ cup water to the sauce, which will have thickened.

Blackberry Cordial

Cordials are simple elixirs, always made from ripe fruit simmered with sugar, and often fortified with brandy, cognac, or other spirits. A little cooking and stirring combined with the passage of time transforms blackberries into a sippable souvenir of summer's fruity bounty, a reason to linger in proximity to a glowing fireplace on a chilly winter evening. Enjoyed since the Renaissance, cordials were once considered to have medicinal value, and often included herbs and spices considered to have healing properties as well as pleasing flavor. Today, cordials serve as treats rather than treatments; and those containing alcohol are simply one type of liqueur.

MAKES ABOUT 3 CUPS

3 cups blackberries

1 cinnamon stick or $\frac{1}{4}$ teaspoon ground cinnamon

7 whole cloves or $\frac{1}{4}$ teaspoon ground cloves

7 whole allspice berries or $\frac{1}{4}$ teaspoon ground allspice

$2\frac{1}{4}$ cups water

1 cup sugar

1 cup brandy or vodka

Combine the berries, spices, and water in a medium saucepan and bring to a lively boil. Adjust the heat to maintain a gentle but active simmer. Cook for 20 minutes. Remove from heat and crush the berries using a potato masher, the back of a slotted spoon, or a fork.

Strain the crushed berries and liquid through a fine-mesh strainer into a medium bowl, leaving the fruit solids, seeds, and whole spices behind. Do not press on the berry pulp; you want only the juice.

Return the strained juice to the saucepan and add the sugar. Bring to a boil over medium-high heat and quickly adjust to maintain a gentle simmer. Cook, stirring occasionally, for 10 minutes to dissolve the sugar. Remove from the heat and cool to room temperature. Add the brandy and stir well.

Pour the cordial into a clean glass jar and seal it tightly. Set aside in a cool, dark place for two to three weeks or up to one year.

Cantaloupe

Driving along a winding Piedmont North Carolina two-lane blacktop sometime in the early 1980s, I saw a large, hand-lettered cardboard sign nailed to a post by the side of the road. Its message, "Western Lopes," made me want to pull over at once, but the pickup truck full of summer fruit had moved on. The abbreviation tickled me, then and now: "'lopes." Spelled variously as "canteloupe," "cantaloupe," and "cantalope," the one true rendering of the name for this summertime delight remains unsettled. The simplicity of the nickname "lopes" cuts through to the subject at hand: a plain, distinctive melon that graces southern plates as the summer heat and humidity reach their peak. Back when eating off the big messy green rind and spitting out the seeds mattered more than flavor, watermelon had my heart; today I am simultaneously a cantaloupe devotee.

Make that a "muskmelon maven," a "rock melon recruit," or perhaps a "Persian melon person," since each of these names belongs to this particular orange-hued, textured-skinned melon, while "cantaloupe," in its various spellings, properly and officially does not. But the mistake was made long ago, a century at least, and with our nationwide affection for these small, round melons, enclosed in a sturdy rind adorned with the distinctive, curling grey-green texture called netting, we've claimed the name for good. In the American South, cantaloupes are what they are, and from July through early September, the sultry-hot South loves her "'lopes."

Native to Iran and traced back to the gardens and tables of ancient Egypt, Greece, and Rome, *Cucumis melo* belongs to the gourd family, and is closely kin to cucumbers and winter melons. Whereas tomatoes, which are technically fruits, are more at home among vegetables, cantaloupes are vegetables that are more at home among fruits. This species of sweet, plump melons found fame and favor in Iran and Armenia around 3000 BCE and made its way throughout Asia and Africa, to Greece and Egypt, and to Rome by the first century of the Common Era.

Here is where the mistaken identity occurred: A smooth-skinned, paler-fleshed variety of *Cucumis melo* found favor in papal gardens near the Italian city of Cantalupo around the sixteenth century, earning it the varietal name *C. melo* var. *cantalupo*. These true cantaloupes, known as charentais and cavaiilon melons, remain hot-weather stars in France and Spain to this day, but they never grew well here in the United States. In contrast, their muskmelon cousin, *Cucumis melo* var. *reticulatus*, grew wonderfully across the pond, especially in the South, and while it was misnamed coming in, it quickly won favor and fame and, for some growers, fortune as well.

Melons receive notice in southern historical accounts of culinary pleasures from colonial times forward, but we can thank the W. Atlee Burpee Company for bringing the particular 'lopes we love to the marketplace in 1881. That year, the "Netted Gem" showed up in their catalogs and found favor around the country, particularly in the South, where heat, sunshine, and sandy soil awaited these summertime beauties.

Traditionally, southerners enjoyed cantaloupes for their own sake, as a sweet, juicy, cool, and refreshing pleasure during the hot and sultry season when they ripen in the heat. Some people, particularly those with a garden's abundance beyond what a family could polish off on its own, turned cantaloupe into jam, preserves, and pickles. But for old-timers, cantaloupes were enough. With twenty-first-century access to prosciutto for wrapping around a ripe crescent of *C. melo* var. *reticulatus*, a blender capable of making smoothies, and a freezer to transform it into sorbet, the South has a whole new reason to love the 'lope.

Cantaloupe Agua Fresca

When the heat and bustle of a summer day becomes a burden, Latin cafés, taquerias, food trucks, and tiendas, have just the solution: huge, barrel-shaped glass jars of agua fresca. They offer a rainbow of liquid refreshment, made from such natural treasures as pineapple, papaya, mango, watermelon, strawberries, hibiscus flowers, and cucumber. Lightly sweetened and often brightened with herbs and lime juice, these beverages distract us from the heat and delight our taste buds. They are refreshing and cool, beautiful to look at, delightful to sip, and so easy to make! If you don't find a source for these refreshing beverages nearby, make some at home. Try it with 4 cups of watermelon, berries, or a mix of fruits, and sweetening it with honey, agave nectar, palm sugar, or any sweetener you prefer.

MAKES 4 SERVINGS

---

1 ripe cantaloupe (about 3 pounds)
3 cups cold water
2–3 tablespoons sugar
2–3 tablespoons fresh lime juice or lemon juice

Wash the cantaloupe well. Cut it in half, remove and discard the seeds, and cut it into 1-inch chunks. You should have about 4 cups.

In the jar of a blender, combine the cantaloupe chunks, 1½ cups of the water, the sugar, and the lime or lemon juice. Process until fairly smooth and well mixed, about 20-30 seconds.

Place a fine mesh strainer over a pitcher or a large mixing bowl. Carefully pour in the cantaloupe mixture. Let the liquids run through and press and scrape well to obtain as much of the juice as possible. Discard the puréed cantaloupe remaining in the strainer. Add the remaining water to the pitcher and stir well. Place in the refrigerator for about 1 hour to chill thoroughly. Serve cold.

Horchata de Melon

This classic Latin beverage makes use of cantaloupe seeds, turning them into a bright, nutty, and delicious drink. How wonderful to learn that the seedy portion of a cantaloupe, which I have always viewed as compost (and once upon a time, as garbage), has culinary possibilities. Horchata is beloved from Central and South America through the Caribbean and Spain, and is often made with raw rice, sesame seeds, coconut, barley, or almonds. Traditional in Mexico, horchata de melon makes the most of the mighty magical melon.

MAKES 1 SERVING

About ½ cup seeds, juice, and pulp from the
    center of 1 ripe cantaloupe
1 cup cold water
2 tablespoons sugar or honey
1 tablespoon fresh lime or lemon juice
Generous pinch of salt

In a blender, combine the cantaloupe seeds, pulp, and juice with the water, sugar or honey, lime or lemon juice, and salt. Blend at high speed for 30 seconds. Stop and scrape down the sides of the blender jar. Blend again for 1 minute, or until the seeds are very finely ground. Pour the contents of the blender jar, seeds and all, into a small bowl or a big glass and chill for at least 1 hour, up to 3 hours. Strain well and then discard the seedy bits left. Pour the liquid over ice and serve cold.

Cantaloupe Preserves

Capture the golden summertime essence of sweet ripe cantaloupe in a jam jar with this simple recipe for old-time preserves. You will need one good-sized cantaloupe or two small ones. But why not double this recipe? You'll have plenty to enjoy for breakfast, lunch, and midnight snack, in addition to making the summer's sweetness something to look forward to come cold weather.

MAKES THREE 4-OUNCE JARS

3 cups cantaloupe chunks ($3\frac{1}{2}$- to 4-pound cantaloupe)
$1\frac{1}{2}$ cups sugar
1 tablespoon fresh lemon juice or lime juice

Prepare three 4-ounce canning jars with tight-fitting lids, washing them in hot soapy water and placing them by the stove. In a medium saucepan, combine the cantaloupe chunks, sugar, and lemon or lime juice. Bring to a rolling boil over medium-high heat, stirring often to help dissolve the sugar. When the mixture has formed a generous amount of syrup, reduce the heat to maintain a gentle simmer. Cook, stirring occasionally, for 3 hours, or until the melon has softened into small pieces and the syrup has thickened into a soft, slightly chunky jam. Set aside to cool to room temperature. When cooled, divide the preserves among the prepared jars and place the lids on top of each jar. Seal tightly and store in the refrigerator for up to 1 week, or process in a hot-water-bath canner to make them shelf-stable. For information on water-bath canning, see page 27.

HOW TO STERILIZE JARS FOR STORING JAMS AND PRESERVES IN THE REFRIGERATOR

To ensure that the jams, jellies, preserves, cordials, and other homemade foods you store are safe and free from microbes, use sturdy jars and lids designed for storing food and sterilize them before use.

Look for sturdy, heatproof glass jars and lids designed for canning and food preservation at hardware stores and many large supermarkets.

To sterilize your jars, place them in a pot large enough to allow water to circulate around them. Place the jars in the pot and add enough water to cover them by 2 inches. Bring the water to a rolling boil over medium heat and boil for 10–12 minutes.

Meanwhile, put the lids and rings in a smaller saucepan with enough water to cover them by 1 inch. Bring the water to a gentle boil, reduce the heat, and a simmer for 10–12 minutes.

While the jars are boiling, place a clean kitchen towel on a countertop where you will be filling the jars. When the time is up, using tongs, carefully remove the jars and place them upside-down to drain on the prepared towel. Transfer the lids and rings to the towel as well.

Prepare the jam or preserves according to the recipe and let it cool to room temperature. Carefully pour or spoon it into the jars, leaving ¼ inch of headroom. Cover each jar with a lid and ring, twisting just enough to tighten it. Label each jar with the contents and date of preparation. Store in the refrigerator for up to 3 weeks.

RESOURCES ON CANNING

Canning is an odd name for the process of creating a shelf-stable environment for jams, jellies, and other foods, given that the finished product goes into glass jars rather than metal cans. But canning is the term, and food safety is key when processing fruit for enjoyment in the future.

Canning is a straightforward process, but it requires special equipment and techniques. The jam and preserves recipes in this book are written for short-term storage in the refrigerator, not long-term storage on a pantry shelf.

To prepare your jams, preserves, and other culinary creations for long-term storage, seek out detailed information before you begin. Here are a few resources offering excellent expert advice on how to process your jars of homemade goodness, so you can enjoy them for up to 1 year:

* Ball Brand Canning / Jarden Home Brands: www.freshpreserving.com, (800) 240-3340
* Canning Across America: www.canningacrossamerica .com
* Food in Jars: www.foodinjars.com
* National Center for Home Food Preservation: nchfp.uga.edu

Sherri Brooks Vinton's
Cantaloupe Pickles

I adore these unexpected pickles, made from the fruit that I tend to lock into a sweet context, limiting its possibilities. My friend Sherri Brooks Vinton thinks creatively and delightfully about flavor and fun, and her books on preserving make me want to head to the farmers' market every weekend and come home with abundant goodness to put up. Sherri suggests an underripe, firm melon for these pickles since they have a long cooking time.

MAKES ABOUT 4 CUPS

1 cantaloupe (to yield 4 cups of 1-inch chunks)

2 cups apple cider vinegar

1 cup sugar

1 tablespoon peeled and grated or very finely chopped
  fresh ginger

2 cinnamon sticks, broken into halves

1 bay leaf, torn in half

3 whole cloves

Wash the cantaloupe well, and then peel it, removing all the rind and seeds. Cut it into 1-inch chunks—you want about 4 cups. In a large nonreactive saucepan, combine all the remaining ingredients. Bring to a boil over medium-high heat and stir well to dissolve the sugar. Remove from the heat and stir in the cantaloupe chunks. Cover and let stand for 1 hour.

Place the pan over medium-high heat and bring to a boil. Lower the heat and cook gently, simmering for 1 hour. The fruit will become translucent.

Transfer the pickles and their cooking liquid to a bowl to cool to room temperature. Then scoop the pickles into jars and add enough cooking liquid to cover them. Cover and refrigerate for up to 3 weeks. For information on water-bath canning, see page 27.

From *Put 'Em Up! A Comprehensive Home Preserving Guide for the Creative Cook* by Sherri Brooks Vinton (North Adams, Mass.: Storey Publishing, 2010).

Cantaloupe Sorbet

With its bright color and pure and refreshing flavor, this cool treat can turn a heat wave into a tropical tea party. A few bites and you'll feel the woes of summer's soaring temperatures melt away. Plan to make the cantaloupe mixture in advance, as the sweetened fruit purée needs at least three hours to chill thoroughly once the it's made. You can make it in the morning and churn it at night. It's best right after you've churned it. If you have extra, freeze it in a shallow pan then break it into chunks and purée it in a food processor to bring back its sorbet texture.

MAKES ABOUT 1 QUART OR 6–8 SERVINGS

½ cup sugar
½ cup water
4 cups peeled chunks of cantaloupe
   (3½- to 4-pound cantaloupe)
1 tablespoon fresh lime juice or lemon juice
¼ teaspoon salt

Make simple syrup by combining the sugar and water in a medium saucepan. Bring to a rolling boil and stir well to dissolve the sugar. Cook, stirring often, until you have a smooth, clear syrup, 2–3 minutes. Remove from the heat, transfer to a small bowl, and chill until very cold, about 1 hour.

Place the fruit in a food processor fitted with the metal blade and, pulsing on and off, grind it into a smooth, evenly textured purée. Add the cold syrup, lime or lemon juice, and salt and process until evenly combined, stopping often to scrape down the sides of the bowl. Transfer to a medium bowl and chill until very cold, at least 3 hours.

Transfer the purée to an ice cream maker and freeze according to the manufacturer's directions. Serve at once.

Damson Plums

Damsons are small, deep-blue, tart-fleshed plums brought to America by English colonists early in the seventeenth century. Traditionally treasured as the key to the finest of plum preserves, damsons have been happily at home in southern soil for more than three centuries. Nursery merchant William Smith of Surry County, Virginia, offered apples, double-blossom peaches, and Damascene plumb among his inventory in 1755, while Thomas Jefferson's legendary gardens at Monticello included two damson plum trees, listed in meticulous records as being planted in 1778 and bearing fruit by 1783.

These dry, ovoid stone-fruits are extremely tart, centered around a large, furrowed, fiercely embedded seed, surrounded by a skimpy amount of extremely dry, astringent flesh. This makes *Prunus domestica* subsp. *Institiia* unsuitable for eating out of hand, drying, or baking into pies and tarts. By macerating them in sugar and simmering them in a preserving pan, a solid, heavy pan with a teacup shape and a heavy bottom, cooks have transformed these petite astringent plums into superb jams, wine, and the fruit paste known as damson cheese, all jewels of both pantry and table.

This fact of requiring cooking surely accounts for their obscurity within the modern family of southern fruits. Peaches, strawberries, watermelons, and figs remain as famous and beloved as they were two centuries ago. We now have more varieties to choose from and know more ways to enjoy them than our ancestors did. We can cook peaches into cobbler and figs into preserves, but we can also pick them up and enjoy their sweet ripeness out of hand: no fuss, no muss. With damsons, only the carefully cultivated and painstakingly transformed into jellies, jams, conserves, and spirits form invited attention, and as modern life moved us farther from farms, and away from tending fruit trees and preserving their yields, the knowledge and affection faded away.

Confusion arises, since the name "damson" is attached to a number of plums, with colors ranging from red to blue and purple to black. Some of these are described as plump, sweet fruits, which are tasty raw as well as cooked. These are not the common damsons long-cherished by southern cooks. To find the common damson, look for petite, dark-blue oval fruits, with a flavor widely described as poor when raw but exceptional when sweetened and cooked.

The names damson and damascene reflect a traditional belief that these plums originated in the Syrian city of Damascus. References to damascene plums in Britain during Roman times show that the Romans imported them from the eastern Mediterranean. But the Romans describe a plump, sweet plum, not the common damson, which requires sugar and heat to shine. Given the similarities between the common damson and the semiwild native *bullace* plums, which thrive in the hedgerows of the English countryside today, researchers consider the common damson to be indigenous to England and Ireland, growing there since ancient times.

I first encountered the common damson in the exquisite and essential cookbook by Edna Lewis, *The Taste of Country Cooking*. In this groundbreaking book, Miss Lewis writes about the damson tree as one of the most beloved in the orchards of Freetown, Virginia, where she was born and raised. She recalls navy-blue plums with purple highlights, small and delicate as bird's eggs. She prefers to leave the pits in the plums throughout the preserving process for the extra flavor they bestowed, and instructs cooks to prick each plum with a sturdy needle to release the juices into the preserving kettle as the cooking process begins. Because I can rely on Edna Lewis's wisdom completely, I knew these little blue jewels were worthy of our attention.

In England common damsons were the plum of choice for the thriving commercial jam industry, which was important until after World War II. In the American South, damsons were always a home-grown fruit, used by families to make preserves for the home pantry. In both cases, changing tastes and the postwar move away from rural living and from cooking and eating with the seasons caused damson trees to fade from awareness and cultivation both. Look for damson plums in farmers' markets and orchards in August and September, and ask around if you don't see them right away. You may want to plant a damson tree or two, for their lovely small white flowers in April and as source and inspiration for making spectacularly tasty jams and preserves.

Damson Plum Jam

Damson plums are indisputably delicious but devilishly difficult to pit. Some old-time cooks solved the problem by leaving the pits in the damsons, knowing that the jam's recipients would consider it worth the trouble to pick them out as they savored the jam. I cook the plums first and then mash the sweet, hot fruit through a sieve or a food mill once the fruit has softened enough to release the pits. Make this jam when you have a stretch of time, since they have to macerate for at least 5 hours.

MAKES ABOUT 3 CUPS
(1½ pints, 3 half-pints, or six 4-ounce jars)

---

2 cups damson plums
2 cups sugar
3 tablespoons fresh lemon juice

Poke the plums several times each with a needle or a skewer. Place them in a medium Dutch oven and cover with the sugar. Stir well and then set aside for at least 5 hours or overnight. Stir occasionally to encourage the plums to release their juices and form a syrup. When you are ready to cook the fruit into jam, prepare jars by sterilizing them (page 26).

Place 2 or 3 saucers in the freezer to use when testing the jam's doneness. Bring the pan of syrupy perforated plums to a lively boil over medium-high heat. Watch carefully and stir often to keep the fruit from scorching. Adjust the heat to maintain a gentle boil. Cook until the plums have softened and the syrup is foamy, pinkish-purple, and abundant, 10–15 minutes. Remove a plum or two to a bowl and mash with a fork. If the pits pop out easily, place a fine-mesh sieve over a medium bowl and pour in the plums and syrup. Press the fruit with the back of a large spoon to release the pits and push the pulp and the softened peel through the mesh and into the bowl. Scrape the rounded bottom of the sieve to be sure you harvest every spoonful of fruit. Discard the pits.

Return the strained pulp and all the juices to the Dutch oven. Add the lemon juice and cook, stirring often, until the jam has thickened and darkened a bit, about 10 minutes. Remove from the heat while you test for doneness. Spoon a tablespoon of the damson liquid onto one of the cold saucers, fresh from the freezer. Does it stay in place rather than running freely? If you push the edge of the liquid with your finger, does it wrinkle a bit? Pull your finger through the liquid. Does it stay separated for a moment or two? If not, return the mixture to the heat and cook about 2 minutes more. Remove from the heat and test again, repeating this process until the jam has thickened up enough to stay in place and wrinkle a bit and a finger run through it leaves a path. Let the jam cool to room temperature. Carefully divide the jam among the sterilized jars, leaving ½ inch of headspace between the surface of the jam and the top of the jar. Cover and refrigerate for 2–3 weeks. For information on water-bath canning, see page 27.

Martha Hall Foose's
Damson Plum Custard Pie

Damson plums challenge those of us who love to bake pies, because their seeds are deeply embedded and quite difficult to extract from the fruit. Their diminutive size adds to the difficulty, since any seed-wrangling must have been done over and over to accumulate enough tart pulp for a properly plummy fruit pie. Hence, this lovely damson plum custard pie makes me deeply happy, relying as it does on seed-free, sweetened damson plum jam. My friend Martha Hall Foose shared this recipe from her Great Aunt Carrye, of Pickens, Mississippi, and it makes a beauty of a pie. I love its lusciousness, with its plummy, jammy custard and bouffant meringue crown.

MAKES ONE 9-INCH PIE

Pastry for a 9-inch single-crust pie (page 38)

FOR THE FILLING
¾ cup sugar
4 tablespoons butter, softened
½ cup damson plum jelly, or another jelly or a seedless jam
½ cup evaporated milk or half-and-half
2 tablespoons all-purpose flour
1 teaspoon pure vanilla extract
½ teaspoon salt
2 large egg yolks
1 large egg

FOR THE MERINGUE
2 large egg whites
4 tablespoons sugar

Heat the oven to 350°. Line a 9-inch pie pan with the rolled-out piecrust. Trim the edges, and fold them or pinch them to make a nice even edge all around the piecrust. Set aside. In a medium bowl, whisk together the sugar and butter. Add the jelly, evaporated milk or half-and-half, flour, vanilla, and salt and stir well.

In a small bowl, combine the egg yolks and whole egg and beat with a fork to mix them well. Add the eggs to the jelly and stir until the ingredients are combined evenly into a smooth, thick filling. Pour the filling into the prepared piecrust.

Place the pie on the bottom shelf of the oven. Bake at 350° until fairly firm, about 25 minutes. Place the pie on a cooling rack or a folded kitchen towel to cool a bit; leave the oven on.

To make the meringue, beat the egg whites in a medium bowl with an electric mixer on medium speed until foamy. Increase the speed to high and add the sugar gradually, about 2 tablespoons at a time. Beat the egg whites until they are thick and shiny and hold curly peaks.

Scoop the meringue onto the filling, mounding it high in the center and spreading it out to meet the crust, leaving no gaps between meringue and crust. Use the back of a spoon to swirl it into curly shapes.

Place the pie on the middle rack of the oven and bake at 350° until the meringue is lightly browned, 12–15 minutes.

Place the pie on a cooling rack or a folded kitchen towel and let cool to room temperature before serving.

HOW TO MAKE PIECRUST FOR A SINGLE-CRUST OR DOUBLE-CRUST PIE

Here is my favorite recipe for piecrust, using butter and a bit of sugar. You can use a pastry blender, a food processor, or your hands to bring these ingredients together into a great crust for your fruit-filled pie. This makes enough pastry for one 9-inch single-crust pie. For a double-crust pie, simply double the recipe. Tightly wrapped, the dough can be refrigerated for up 2 days or frozen for up 2 months.

FOR A SINGLE-CRUST PIE
$1\frac{1}{4}$ cups all-purpose flour
$1\frac{1}{2}$ teaspoons sugar
$\frac{1}{2}$ teaspoon salt
6 tablespoons cold butter, cut into $\frac{1}{2}$-inch chunks
4–6 tablespoons ice-cold water

FOR A DOUBLE-CRUST PIE
$2\frac{1}{2}$ cups all-purpose flour
1 tablespoon sugar
1 teaspoon salt
12 tablespoons cold butter ($\frac{3}{4}$ cup), cut into $\frac{1}{2}$-inch chunks
8–12 tablespoons ($\frac{1}{2}$–$\frac{3}{4}$ cup) ice-cold water

In a food processor work bowl, combine the flour, sugar, and salt. Process for 10 seconds and then pulse on and off to combine the dry ingredients well. Add the butter and process for 15 seconds. Pulse on and off just until the mixture has a rough texture with small pea-sized bits of butter still visible.

With the motor running, add 4 tablespoons of the cold water all at once. Stop and scrape down the sides of the bowl. Pulse on and off to evenly combine the liquid with the flour and butter. As soon as the dough holds together well and is even-textured and smooth, turn it out onto a floured countertop. Quickly shape it into a disk about 6 inches in diameter (or two disks if you are making a double-crust batch) and wrap in waxed paper or plastic wrap. Chill for at least 30 minutes and up to 2 days, or wrap it tightly in plastic wrap and freeze for up to 3 months.

To roll out the piecrust, place a chilled disk of piecrust on the counter and let it warm up for about 10 minutes. Unwrap and place the disk on a generously floured surface. Using a rolling pin so that it is parallel to the edge of the counter, and starting from the center of the disk, roll the dough away from you, pressing firmly. Return the rolling pin to the center and roll toward you. Placing the rolling pin perpendicular to the counter, roll the dough from the center to the left, and then from the center to the right. Gently turn the somewhat flattened disk a quarter turn to the right. Repeat, rolling and pressing the dough out into an even sheet of piecrust, turning often, lifting gently to do so, until your circle is about 10 inches in diameter. To store, place the piecrust circle between two sheets of waxed paper, parchment paper, or plastic wrap, and roll it into a cylinder. Repeat the rolling instructions with the second disk if making a double-crust pie. Refrigerate or freeze until needed, or use at once, fitting it into a pie pan or over a filled fruit piecrust. Alternatively, you can fit the piecrust into a pie pan, crimp the top edges of the crust, and then freeze. Once frozen, wrap airtight, using plastic wrap or aluminum foil. Use frozen in recipes—no need to thaw before filling and baking.

Lamb Shanks with Damson Plum Sauce

This dish requires time and attention, but this investment on your part will be generously rewarded with a hearty, memorable, and abundantly delicious pot of stew. The lamb shanks are browned and then braised in a sauce made with Moroccan-inspired spices and damson plum jam. Lamb shanks vary in size, with the fore shanks being larger than the hind shanks. With smaller shanks, you can serve them on the bone. With larger shanks, you could pull the tender meat off the bones and serve it as a chunky stew. Plan on a means of savoring the wonderful sauce. Options include couscous, rice, mashed potatoes, noodles, or warm flatbread.

MAKES 4 SERVINGS

- 2 teaspoons ground cumin
- 1 teaspoon ground cinnamon
- 1 teaspoon ground ginger
- $\frac{1}{2}$ teaspoon ground coriander
- 4 lamb shanks (about $5\frac{1}{2}$ pounds, total)
- $1\frac{1}{2}$ teaspoons salt
- 1 teaspoon freshly ground black or white pepper
- 3 tablespoons olive oil
- 2 cups chopped onion
- 2 tablespoons chopped garlic
- 3 cups chicken stock
- $\frac{3}{4}$ cup damson plum jam (page 34)
- $\frac{1}{3}$ cup chopped flat-leaf or curly parsley
- Rice or couscous, for serving (optional)

In a small bowl, combine the cumin, cinnamon, ginger, and coriander and stir with a fork to mix them well. Set aside by the stove.

Place a platter by the stove to hold the lamb shanks as you brown them. Heat the oil in a large Dutch oven over medium-high heat. Season the lamb shanks with the salt and pepper. Add a bit of garlic, and if it sizzles immediately, add two of the lamb shanks and let them brown nicely, turning once, about 5 minutes. Transfer to the platter and brown the remaining lamb shanks.

Lower the heat to medium and add the onions to the pan. Cook, tossing often, until they are fragrant, about 2 minutes. Add the garlic and cook until it releases its aroma. Add the spice mixture and toss to mix it with the onions. Cook, stirring often, until the onions are shiny and tender, about 2 minutes more.

Add the chicken stock and damson plum jam and increase the heat to medium high. Stir well to help the jelly dissolve into the sauce. Return the lamb shanks to the pan and let the sauce come to a boil. Adjust the heat to maintain a lively simmer, cover, and cook for 1½–2 hours, checking now and then, turning the lamb shanks once so that they cook evenly. Continue cooking until the meat is very tender and easily pulled from the bones. Remove from the heat and check the seasoning, adding salt if need be. Stir in the parsley. If you're boning the lamb, before serving, use forks or tongs to coax the meat from the bones in large chunks. Discard the bones and transfer the lamb to a serving bowl along with the sauce. If you're not boning the lamb, serve the individual lamb shanks over rice or couscous, with generous portions of sauce over each shank.

Figs

Among all the fruits southerners hold dear, none originates earlier in human history than the fig. Evidence of figs' existence in the wild in Africa, the Middle East, and South Asia goes back millennia, including sites near the ancient city of Jericho. Cultivated in antiquity in the Mediterranean and what is now Iran, Afghanistan, and India, they were valued in ancient Greece and Rome not only as a delicious and accessible food but also as objects of beauty. They are featured in frescoes and appear as poetic symbols of comfort and prosperity in literature, including the Bible and the Koran.

Introduced to the Americas by Spaniards exploring what is now Florida in the sixteenth century, *Ficus carica* took to the southern climate. Figs love heat and sunshine, so the fast-growing, large-leaved, low-maintenance, and prolific fruit trees quickly took root. Fig orchards thrived at Mount Vernon and Monticello, with the Marseilles variety noted as flourishing in both historic Virginia locations.

Fig trees thrive in varying climates all over the South, except where long, hard freezes are part of the picture. Coastal communities from Texas and Louisiana up to Virginia and Maryland have been fig-friendly locales for centuries, and inland up to the mountain South, you'll find recipes for fig preserves, jams, relishes, cookies, and cakes in cookbooks both historical and modern.

Though viable and appreciated throughout the American South for nearly three centuries, figs were never commercially important outside their immediate growing area. This is because their thin skin and soft, delicate texture makes them poor candidates for shipping and storing. But at home in the South, the small sweet southern fig has been a home-grown pleasure for hundreds of years.

Today, figs from California are widely available seasonally in supermarkets throughout the South. As in most of the United States, the best-known fig product throughout the South is the Fig Newton, which originated in Newton, Massachusetts in the early twentieth century and is made with dried figs rather than fresh. Until fig growers overcame the challenges of shipping figs throughout the country, most Americans had only tasted dried figs, and usually in the form of those ubiquitous sturdy, square, filled cookies.

The proliferation of farmers' markets, CSAs (Community Supported Agriculture), and locally oriented chefs, cooks, and eaters around the South since the 1990s, has given local growers a way to offer old-school figs to a grateful southern public. Celeste and brown turkey are the most common southern cultivars, and they grow on low, leafy bushes. If you're inclined to grow fruit in your southern yard, garden, or farmstead, consider figs. They've obviously stood the test of time, and they're self-pollinating, which means you only need one tree or bush. They don't have thorns and require little fuss, as long as you plant them in a sunny spot, ideally near a wall or fence. Plan to share your fig tree's bounty with neighboring wildlife, because birds and other creatures share our appreciation of this ancient treat. You could plant a green variety, since these are said to discourage visitors, given that the ripe figs don't show up like the classic dark brown and purple classics, or you could just share!

Be ready to pick and enjoy your figs immediately once their season arrives, because they ripen in abundance. If you don't feel like making jam, just get some prosciutto, honey, cheese, and wine, sweet tea, or lemonade, and invite friends over to help you handle the blessing. To capture the abundance once they come in, take the expert advice of Andrea Weigl, author of *Pickles & Preserves: A Savor the South Cookbook* (University of North Carolina Press, 2014): Wash and dry them gently, and cut away their stems. Place the figs whole in plastic freezer bags (pint- or quart-size make a convenient amount), and freeze. To make jam or preserves, use them straight from the freezer.

Fig Preserves

*From Virginia to Florida, North Carolina to Louisiana or any-
where in the sunniest southern states, when figs get ripe, even
people who don't garden to fill a winter pantry may haul out
the kettle and make fig preserves. This is because figs come in in
an abundant rush, faster than most of us can eat them up. They
need to ripen on the tree or bush, which means that even with the
birds and four-legged creatures competing for the crop, it's easy
to have more than we can enjoy fresh. Fig preserves have just a
few ingredients, and they wonderfully capture this unique fruit's
flavor and texture. Best of all, though, preserved figs are the ticket
to Ocracoke Island Fig Cake (page 52). Traditionally, cooks leave
the stems on, but it's fine to remove them before you begin to cook.*

MAKES ABOUT 3 PINT JARS OR ABOUT 5 HALF-PINT JARS

---

3 pounds fresh, ripe whole figs
3 cups sugar
3 lemon slices
½ cup water

Prepare canning jars by following the instructions on page 26.

Gently rinse the figs in cool water and transfer to large
cooking pot, such as an enamel cast-iron Dutch oven. (The figs
should fill the pan only halfway so they have room to simmer.)
Add the sugar, lemon slices, and water, and stir gently to mix
them well. Place over medium-high heat and bring to a boil.
Quickly lower the heat, adjusting it to maintain an active,
visible simmer.

Cook, stirring occasionally, for 1 hour and 15 minutes, or
until the figs are very tender and surrounded by a nice thick,
flavorful syrup.

Remove from the heat and let cool to room temperature.
Transfer to the prepared jars and cover tightly with lids. Store
in the refrigerator for 2–3 weeks.

Vimala Rajendran's Fig Compote

This vibrant accompaniment to both savory and sweet dishes comes from the chef/owner of Vimala's Curryblossom Café in Chapel Hill, North Carolina. Typical of the flavor-packed, irresistible menu her customers adore, this luscious dish is part of Vimala's solution to the abundance of sweet, ripe fruit on the fig tree in her backyard. Serve this as you would chow-chow or pickles, dolloping it on a plate of sliced tomatoes, corn-on-the-cob, green beans, new potatoes, and fried okra. Or celebrate its sweetness by spooning some over vanilla ice cream or a bowl of yogurt or oatmeal.

MAKES 4–6 SERVINGS

---

1 pound fresh, ripe figs (about 24 medium-sized figs)
$1/4$ cup dark or light brown sugar, lightly packed
1 cup dry sherry
1 lemon, quartered and thinly sliced, seeds removed
$1/2$ teaspoon salt

Remove and discard the stem from each fig. Quarter the figs lengthwise and set aside.

In a medium saucepan, combine the brown sugar, sherry, and lemon slices. Place over medium-high heat and cook, stirring often, until the mixture becomes a thin syrup.

Add the figs, reduce the heat to maintain a lively simmer, and cook until the figs are glossy and the syrup thickens a bit, about 2 minutes more.

Remove the pan from the heat, stir in the salt, and transfer the compote to a medium bowl to cool. Serve warm or at room temperature. To store, cool the compote completely, place it in a container, cover, and refrigerate for up to 3 days.

Fresh Fig Chutney with Cilantro and Toasted Cumin

This simple chutney makes a fine accompaniment to grilled meats, roasted vegetables, curry-centered meals, or sandwiches in need of a hearty, flavor-packed kick. It's outstanding as a flavorful accent to any pasta- or rice-focused meal. If you don't have a food processor or a blender, finely chop the figs and mash them by hand to make a soft texture. You can use any ripe fresh figs for this chutney, including Alma, brown turkey, Celeste, Kadota, magnolia, or any diminutive southern figs.

MAKES ABOUT 2 CUPS

---

1 dozen small fresh figs (about 2½ cups loosely packed)

1 tablespoon chopped garlic

½ cup white wine, such as Sauvignon Blanc or Chardonnay

2 teaspoons ground cumin

3 tablespoons apple cider vinegar

1 tablespoon fresh lemon juice

1 teaspoon salt

½ teaspoon cayenne pepper

¼ cup chopped fresh cilantro

Cilantro leaves, for garnish

Remove and discard the stems from the figs, and chop them very coarsely. Transfer the figs to the work bowl of a food processor or the jar of a blender. Add the garlic and wine and pulse to chop them into a chunky sauce. Scrape this mixture into a large bowl and set aside.

In a small skillet, toast the cumin over medium-high heat just until it darkens a little and is fragrant. Add the cumin, vinegar, lemon juice, salt, cayenne, and cilantro to the figs. Stir to mix everything together evenly and well.

Taste and adjust the seasonings if needed. Transfer to a small bowl and top with a few cilantro leaves. Serve immediately or cover and chill for up to 2–3 days.

Fresh Fig Pie

This pie showcases the rich, elegant, rustic nature of sweet figs and is an excellent solution to an excess of very ripe figs at the height of the season. While ice cream is not essential, it makes an extraordinary partner for this timeless dessert.

MAKES ONE 9-INCH PIE

Pastry for a 9-inch double-crust pie (page 38)

½ cup sugar

2 tablespoons all-purpose flour

½ teaspoon ground cinnamon

½ teaspoon salt

4 cups very coarsely chopped fresh, ripe figs
   (about 1½ pounds)

2 tablespoons fresh lemon juice, cider vinegar,
   or white vinegar

1 tablespoon cold butter, cut into bits

Heat the oven to 375°. Line a 9-inch pie pan with one of the rolled-out piecrusts. In a small bowl, combine the sugar, flour, cinnamon, and salt and stir with a fork to mix well. Place the figs in a medium bowl and add the sugar mixture; toss gently to mix them evenly. Pour the figs into the piecrust and mound them up toward the center in to a little pile. Pour the lemon juice or vinegar over the figs and dot with the butter.

Cover with the second rolled-out piecrust and press the edges of both crusts together to seal them well. Trim and fold the edges under firmly, then crimp to seal the pie, or press the edges down with the tines of a fork to seal them and make a pretty design. Use a fork or a knife to make steam vents in the crust so that steam and juicy filling can escape as the pie cooks.

Bake for 10 minutes. Reduce the temperature to 350° and bake until the filling is thick and juicy and bubbling out around the top of the pie and the crust is golden brown, 45–50 minutes. Transfer to a cooling rack or a folded kitchen towel to cool. Serve warm or at room temperature.

Ocracoke Island Fig Cake
with Buttermilk Glaze

This signature cake makes use of the luscious figs that ripen in midsummer on this barrier island in North Carolina's Outer Banks. Most local residents have a backyard tree or two, and many are dedicated to eating what they can through the season and canning the rest. For this recipe, use whole preserved figs, which you drain, stem, and chop into ½-inch chunks. Another option is to use prepared fig jam, which needs no chopping. To use dried figs, see Note.

MAKES ONE 10-INCH CAKE

FOR THE CAKE

3 large eggs

1½ cups sugar

1 cup vegetable oil

2 cups all-purpose flour

1 teaspoon ground nutmeg

1 teaspoon ground allspice

1 teaspoon ground cinnamon

1 teaspoon salt

1 teaspoon baking soda dissolved in a little hot water

½ cup buttermilk (or see Note)

1 teaspoon pure vanilla extract

1 cup coarsely chopped preserved figs (page 46), or fig jam
   (see Note regarding use of dried figs)

1 cup coarsely chopped pecans or walnuts

1/2 cup buttermilk (see Note)
1/2 cup sugar
4 tablespoons butter
1 1/2 teaspoons cornstarch or all-purpose flour, divided
1/4 teaspoon baking soda
1 teaspoon pure vanilla extract

To make the cake, heat the oven to 350°. Grease and flour a
10-inch tube cake pan or Bundt pan and set aside. Beat the eggs
well until light yellow and smooth. Add the sugar and oil and
continue beating well to make a thick, smooth mixture.

Combine the flour with the nutmeg, allspice, cinnamon,
and salt in a small bowl, and stir to mix well. Add half the flour
mixture to the egg-and-sugar mixture and stir well. Add the
buttermilk and mix well. Add the remaining flour along with the
baking soda dissolved in water and the vanilla, and stir to mix
everything into a fairly smooth batter. Gently stir in the figs and
the nuts, mixing just until they are evenly distributed throughout the batter.

Quickly scrape the batter into the prepared pan, and bake at
350° for 40–50 minutes, or until the cake is handsomely brown
and firm on top, and a wooden skewer inserted in the cake
comes out clean. While the cake bakes, prepare the buttermilk
glaze and set aside until the cake is done.

Cool the cake in the pan on a wire rack, or folded kitchen
towel for about 15 minutes. Loosen the cake from the pan gently,
using a table knife to go around the sides of the pan, and then
gently turn it out onto the wire rack. Turn cake topside up, and

carefully place it on a serving plate or cake stand. Spoon the buttermilk glaze over the warm cake, and cool completely. To make the glaze, in a medium saucepan, combine the buttermilk, sugar, butter, cornstarch, and baking soda, and bring to a gentle boil. Remove at once, stir well, and cool to room temperature. Add the vanilla, and set aside until the cake is done.

NOTE ❋ If you don't have buttermilk, stir 1 tablespoon of vinegar into 1 cup of milk and let stand for 10 minutes.

To use dried figs in this recipe (available in many supermarkets and Middle Eastern and South Asian grocery stores), stem them, halve them lengthwise, and combine them in a medium saucepan with 1 cup of water and 1 cup of sugar. Bring to a boil over medium-high heat. Stir well and reduce the heat to maintain a visible simmer. Cook gently for about 30 minutes. Cool to room temperature. Remove the figs from the syrup, chop them, and return them to the syrup until needed for the cake.

Loella Fugate's Fig Swirl Cookies

My friend Jill Warren Lucas cherishes this recipe because it came from a precious source: her husband Tim's grandmother, who passed away in 1992. Loella Fugate loved cooking and especially baking and bequeathed her recipe box to Jill, who describes it wonderfully: "Her recipe collection is a treasure. A basic wooden box with rich grain marks and tongue-in-groove corners. Most of the cards show her familiar looping handwriting and scant directions, relics of an era where precise details were not needed, as all housewives knew their way around a kitchen." Mrs. Fugate's original recipe calls for chopped dates, which make a fine cookie, but I use chopped dried figs with wonderful results. These take a while to assemble, with time out for chilling the dough, so bake them when you have some time to enjoy the process.

MAKES ABOUT 4 DOZEN

FOR THE FILLING

2 cups chopped dried figs (about 8 ounces)
$\frac{1}{2}$ cup sugar
$\frac{3}{4}$ cup water
1 tablespoon Cointreau (optional)

FOR THE COOKIE DOUGH

2 cups cake flour
$\frac{1}{2}$ teaspoon salt
$\frac{1}{2}$ teaspoon baking soda
$\frac{1}{2}$ cup (1 stick) unsalted butter, softened
$\frac{1}{2}$ cup granulated sugar
$\frac{1}{2}$ cup light brown sugar, lightly packed
1 large egg
$\frac{1}{2}$ teaspoon lemon extract

To make the filling, combine the figs, sugar, and water in a medium saucepan. Bring to a gentle boil over medium-high heat. Stir well and then reduce the heat to maintain a lively simmer. Cook, stirring often, until the mixture is thick and jammy, about 7 minutes. Remove from the heat and stir in the Cointreau, if using. Set aside to cool while you make the cookie dough.

In a medium bowl, whisk together the flour, salt, and baking soda. In a large bowl, combine the butter, granulated sugar, and brown sugar. Using an electric mixer or a whisk, beat at high speed until soft, creamy, and well-combined. Add the egg and lemon extract and beat well, stopping to scrape the bowl now and then. Continue beating until the ingredients come together into a creamy, fluffy mixture.

Add the flour mixture and stir to combine. Continue mixing, using the spoon or your hands, until you have a smooth, sturdy dough.

Turn the dough out onto a large piece of parchment or waxed paper. Pat and the press the dough into a big rectangle. Cover the dough with another piece of parchment or waxed paper and gently roll it into a loose roll. Refrigerate until it is very cool and firm, about 45 minutes.

Unroll the dough, remove it from the parchment or waxed paper, and place it on a lightly floured counter or cutting board. Cut the dough into two rectangles and roll each out to measure about 6 by 8 inches.

Transfer one of the rectangles back to the parchment paper and continue rolling until it measures about 8 by 10 inches. With the longer edges of the dough facing you, spread or crumble half of the fig mixture over the dough, leaving about an inch of bare dough along the edge closest to you. Using the parchment paper to help, starting with the edge farthest from you, roll the dough, as tight as you can, toward you to make a log shape. Repeat with the remaining dough and filling. Wrap the rolls in parchment paper and refrigerate for at least 2 hours or overnight.

When the logs are cold and firm and you are ready to bake, heat the oven to 375°. Grease a cookie sheet or line it with parchment paper. Cut the logs crosswise into ¼-inch-thick slices and place them about 1 inch apart on the prepared cookie sheet. Bake until the cookies have puffed up, turned a handsome golden-brown, and become fragrant, 8–10 minutes. Transfer to a cooling rack or a platter to cool to room temperature. Store the cookies in an airtight container for up to 4 days.

Mayhaws

The mayhaw is the one southern fruit in this book that was brand new to me going in. This deciduous, prolific member of the hawthorn family grows wild in the wetlands of Arkansas, East Texas, Florida, Louisiana, Mississippi, and Georgia. Mayhaws flourish in swamps, on riverbanks, and along creeks. Mayhaw trees fill out their bare, thorny branches with lovely white-to-pink blossoms early in the spring, developing beautiful bright red fruit in late April and May. Since *Crataegus aestivalis* grows from seed, trees tend to cluster in groves, making them attractive destinations for wildlife during their brief season each spring.

Their preference for riverbanks makes them a challenge, but not an insurmountable one, for mayhaw gatherers. Many families from regions where they thrive have long made springtime mayhaw foraging expeditions a tradition. Elders reminisce about annual outings in small boats, during which everyone gathers ripe mayhaws from the surface of the water using nets and buckets.

Unlike blackberry picking or wild strawberry gathering, collecting mayhaws seldom involves chiding children and adults to stop eating up what they've gathered. Mayhaws are small, cylindrical fruits, less than an inch in length, thin-skinned and endowed with a few seeds. They resemble cherries from a distance but look more like tiny apples when cut open and examined up close. Like quince, they are tart and unappealing when raw, but when transformed into juice, jelly, syrup, or wine, the multigenerational passion for mayhaws and dedication to gathering them becomes clear. With a bit of cooking to coax out their colorful juice and an infusion of sugar, mayhaws, which are rich in pectin, become a beautiful translucent sunset-pink jelly that's luminous, tangy, and perfect for enjoying on a hot buttered biscuit.

Old-timers knew to head out on a reconnaissance mission toward the end of winter in order to spot the flowers and plan their May harvesting destinations. Mayhaw blossoms precede the leaves and, from a distance, look like magical snowflakes frozen and floating in the air. Bees produce mayhaw-inspired honey, and mayhaw's fans hold annual mayhaw festivals in towns across their growing region, including Colquitt, Georgia; Daisett, Texas; El Dorado, Arkansas; and two Louisiana communities, Marion and Starks.

Despite the long traditions of mayhaw gathering and preserving, and the profusion of mayhaw trees in the wild, the indigenous southern fruit is threatened by development, which has caused the swift and ongoing destruction of wetlands, woodlands, and wild stretches of river, creeks, and swamplands. Slow Food USA, an international organization of people dedicated to preserving and celebrating traditional agriculture, sustainability, and food production, has added mayhaw jelly and syrup to its list of endangered foods, plants, and food products, due to the devastating effects of deforestation, clear-cutting, and diseases on wild mayhaw trees, and the loss of access to the trees by boat in the traditional way. Without our ability to forage among the wild trees, the longtime traditions of turning each season's fruit into traditional artisan foods could disappear in less than a generation.

Fortunately, since their beauty and attractiveness to wildlife makes them a prized ornamental tree for landscaping as well as fruit harvesting, mayhaw trees have been cultivated and planted in orchards in the South since the 1800s. To harvest mayhaws from orchards, savvy fans place big tarps out under the trees at harvest time and shake the trees to release the ripe fruit, just as mayhaw fans do from their boats in the wild.

Chefs, home cooks, and mixologists have opened up the mayhaw's culinary potential in recent years, using mayhaw juice and jelly in vinaigrettes, marinades, barbecue sauce, baking, and cocktails.

I have yet to hunker down in a small boat on a May morning for a mayhaw adventure, but I hope to do so in the not-too-distant future. I have been lucky enough to savor mayhaw jelly and juice, and its extraordinary flavor and vivid jewel color, as well as its history that reminds us to go slowly and enjoy seasonal pleasures, has made me a fan. I didn't grow up with mayhaws, but I support all efforts to ensure that they remain a part of the southern culinary landscape—in the wild, in the backyard, on the stove, and between the biscuits—for generations to come.

Mayhaw Jelly

Mayhaws are gorgeous and flavorful, easy to love but difficult to find, so it makes sense to capture their goodness in a lasting way. Mayhaw jelly does that wonderfully, turning an edible but not-so-delicious fruit into a jewel-colored essence of sweet-and-tangy goodness. Mayhaw jelly–making requires two steps: first, turning the crab-apple-like fruit into juice, and then cooking the juice with sugar to make a lovely jelly. The Louisiana State University Agricultural Center has been a cheerleader and research engine on behalf of mayhaw cultivation in recent years, and this recipe is based on their instructions for making jelly from the southern gem. You can start with fruit as directed or order mayhaw juice and begin with the second section below on turning the juice into mayhaw jelly.

MAKES SIX HALF-PINT OR TWELVE 4-OUNCE JARS

2½ pounds of mayhaws (2 quarts)
Water to cover (about 6 cups)
6 tablespoons powdered pectin
5½ cups sugar

Prepare the mayhaws by sorting them to remove any leaves and inedible bits. Leave their tiny stems and blossom in place, as you will be straining the fruit after cooking. Combine the mayhaws and water in a large Dutch oven or stockpot and bring to a boil. Adjust the heat to maintain a simmer and cook for 30 minutes. Set aside to cool and then strain the mixture through a colander into a large bowl. Press gently on the cooked fruit with the back of a spoon to extract the juice.

Discard the fruit and line the colander with three thicknesses of cheesecloth. Strain the juice through the cloth and discard any sediment left behind. You should have about 6 cups of juice, of which you will need 4 cups to make the jelly. Freeze the remaining juice for your next batch of mayhaw jelly.

Prepare the jars for the jelly as directed on page 26.

In a large Dutch oven or stockpot, dissolve the pectin in the mayhaw juice. Bring the juice to a rolling boil over high heat, stirring now and then, and add the sugar. Stir well to dissolve the sugar. Bring the mixture back to a full rolling boil (you will know it is boiling hard enough when the liquid rises to the top of the pot and cannot be stirred down). Boil hard for 1 minute and 15 seconds, stirring often and well.

Remove from the heat and skim off any foam on the surface with a spoon. Carefully pour the hot liquid into the prepared jars, leaving about ¼ inch headroom between jelly and lid. Let cool to room temperature. Cover with lids, seal, and store in the refrigerator for up to 3 weeks.

Mayhaw Jelly–Glazed Shrimp with Zucchini

This simple stir-fry makes a gorgeous dish, with plump pink shrimp tumbled with green triangles of zucchini in a rosy and tangy mayhaw-infused sauce. Everything cooks quickly, tossed in a wok or a big, deep skillet. In place of the zucchini, you can use strips of red, green, or yellow bell pepper, trimmed snow peas, or lightly cooked asparagus cut into 1-inch lengths. Serve this with rice, couscous, or orzo, or toss it with linguine for a pasta feast.

MAKES 3–4 SERVINGS WITH RICE, PASTA, OR GRAINS

- 2 small or 1 medium zucchini
- 2 tablespoons vegetable oil
- ½ cup chopped onion
- 1 tablespoon chopped garlic
- ¾ pound medium to large shrimp, peeled and deveined
- ⅓ cup mayhaw jelly
- 1 teaspoon soy sauce
- 1 teaspoon salt
- ½ teaspoon freshly ground black or white pepper
- 3 green onions, white portion minced, green portion cut in 1-inch lengths

Prepare the zucchini by trimming away the stem end and base. Cut lengthwise into quarters, and then chop each long section into small triangles, about ¼ inch thick. Measure out and prepare all the remaining ingredients and place by the stove, along with a serving platter.

Heat the oil over medium-high heat until a bit of garlic added to the oil sizzles immediately. Add the onions and cook, tossing often, until they are shiny and fragrant, about 1 minute. Add the garlic and toss well. Push the onions and garlic to the sides of the pan and add the shrimp, spreading them around the hot pan's surface in a single layer to cook on one side until bright pink, about 1 minute. Toss everything together well and cook until the shrimp is pink and firm, and then add the zucchini. Toss well and cook 1 minute. Add the mayhaw jelly, soy sauce, salt, and pepper and toss well. Cook, tossing now and then, until the zucchini is tender and the seasonings form a simple sauce, about 1 minute more. Add the green onions and toss well. Transfer to the serving platter and serve hot.

Mayhaw Meatballs

If you love Swedish meatballs and other hearty party variations on the meatball theme, you will love this dish. Mayhaw jelly shares a tart, bright flavor and rosy hue with lingonberry jelly, a traditional accompaniment to Swedish meatballs, so this riff on the Scandinavian classic came to mind. Stirred into the sauce, mayhaw jelly provides marvelous sweet-and-sour notes. While these meatballs will disappear as a tooth-pick-ready party snack, consider making them for a proper meal, served traditionally with boiled potatoes, or tossed with curly egg noodles or linguine for a tangy spin on spaghetti and meatballs.

MAKES 24–26 MEATBALLS

⅓ cup bread crumbs
1 teaspoon salt
½ teaspoon freshly ground black or white pepper
½ teaspoon ground allspice
½ teaspoon ground nutmeg
2 tablespoons butter or vegetable oil
½ cup chopped onion
1 large egg, beaten well
2 tablespoons milk
1 pound ground beef
3 tablespoons butter
2 tablespoons all-purpose flour
2 cups chicken stock or beef broth
2 tablespoons chopped parsley
½ cup mayhaw jelly
½ cup sour cream

In a large bowl, combine the bread crumbs, salt, pepper, allspice, and nutmeg. Use a fork to mix them together well. Heat the butter or oil in a small skillet over medium-high heat until sizzling and bubbling hot. Add the onions and cook, stirring often, until they are fragrant, shiny, and wilting, about 3 minutes.

Add the onions, egg, milk, and ground beef to the bread-crumb mixture. Using a large spoon or your hands, stir and scoop to combine everything evenly and well.

Using your hands, form the meat mixture into 1-inch balls and place them on a large platter. You should have about 24 meatballs. Set the remain ingredients and another large platter by the stove.

To cook the meatballs, heat the butter in a large, deep skillet or a small Dutch oven over medium-high heat. When the butter has melted and is sizzling and bubbling hot, add about half the meatballs. Cook, turning as needed, until they are evenly browned. They need not be done, as they will finish cooking in the sauce. Transfer the browned meatballs to the platter and cook the remaining meatballs.

When all the meatballs are browned, add the flour to the fat in the pan. Cook, stirring often, until the flour is lightly browned and smoothly combined. Add the chicken stock or beef broth and bring to a boil, stirring often. When the ingredients have come together into a smooth sauce that has thickened a bit, return the meatballs to the pan. Cook, stirring gently now and then, until the meatballs are cooked through and the sauce has thickened to smooth gravy, 8–10 minutes. Scoop the meatballs out into a serving bowl, leaving the sauce in the pan. Add the mayhaw jelly to the sauce and stir well with a whisk until the jelly melts into the sauce. Remove from the heat and whisk in the sour cream and then the parsley. Pour the sauce over the meatballs in the serving bowl and serve hot or warm.

Slow-Cooker Pulled Pork with Mayhaw Jelly Barbecue Sauce

Put this hearty party centerpiece on to cook and then go about your business, tending to your daily routines or sleeping the night away. Eight hours later, you'll have an abundance of tender, flavorful pork, ready to tuck into buns with tangy, chili-kissed slaw, or tuck into tortillas for taco night. You could also let it cool, cover and chill it, and then heat it up for a fast, fresh feast the next day. Pork shoulder is just what its name implies. Pork shoulder is mysteriously often labeled pork butt, which it isn't, but never mind. By either name, it's rich and flavorful meat, the traditional choice for North Carolina's famous hickory-smoked, Lexington-style chopped barbecue.

MAKES 8–10 SERVINGS

FOR THE PORK

1 tablespoon vegetable oil

1 tablespoon plain or smoked paprika

1 teaspoon ground cumin

1 teaspoon ground ginger

1 teaspoon salt

1 teaspoon freshly ground black or white pepper

1/2 teaspoon cayenne pepper

1 cup finely chopped onions

1 tablespoon finely chopped garlic

3 1/2 pounds boneless pork shoulder

1/2 cup chicken stock

FOR THE BARBECUE SAUCE

1 tablespoon plain or smoked paprika

1 tablespoon ground cumin

2 teaspoons ground ginger

1 teaspoon cayenne pepper

1½ teaspoons salt

1 teaspoon freshly ground black or white pepper

1 cup Mayhaw Jelly (page 62)

⅓ cup apple cider vinegar or white vinegar

¼ cup ketchup

2 tablespoons brown sugar, lightly packed

2 teaspoons soy sauce

Grease the slow cooker with the vegetable oil and add the onions and garlic. Combine the paprika, cumin, ginger, salt, pepper, and cayenne in a small bowl and stir with a fork to mix well. Sprinkle the spice mixture over the pork and use your hands to rub the seasoning over the meat. Place the pork in the slow cooker and add the chicken stock. Cover and cook on low for 8 hours or on high for about 4 hours.

Meanwhile, prepare the barbecue sauce. In a medium bowl, combine the paprika, cumin, ginger, cayenne, salt, and pepper. Use a whisk or a fork to mix them well. Add the mayhaw jelly, vinegar, ketchup, brown sugar, and soy sauce. Stir vigorously with a whisk, bringing everything together evenly into a smooth, thick sauce. You will have about 1¾ cups of sauce. When the meat is cooked through and tender enough to pull apart easily, transfer it from the slow cooker to a platter. Remove and discard the fat. Pour the cooking liquid into a medium saucepan and skim off and discard the fat on the surface. Bring to a lively boil and cook, stirring now and then, until thickened, 5–10 minutes.

Meanwhile, using two forks, tongs, or your hands, pull the pork into shreds and small chunks. Pour the cooking liquid over the shredded pork. Toss to mix well. Add about ¾ cup of the barbecue sauce and toss again to season the meat evenly and well. Cover and refrigerate the remaining barbecue sauce for another meal. Taste the pork and adjust the salt if needed. Serve hot or warm.

Muscadine and Scuppernong Grapes

Riding along a country road in Piedmont North Carolina on a wintry afternoon, I look behind the older houses, hoping to see what you might take for T-post clotheslines at first glance but are shorter in length and height and made of chunky wood rather than metal. And the rows of wires strung over the tops don't wait for damp shirts and pillowcases. These are homemade grape arbors, built to support the curving tendrils and big, floppy leaves of native grapevines, which will awaken come spring and offer up their annual abundance of scuppernongs. These fat, round, gold to bronze native grapes once decorated the summer landscape of many a southern home, providing shade, beauty, and an early fall sweet treat for eating out of hand. With their cousins, dark purple-blue muscadine grapes, which are often found in the wild, they are the starting point for more deliciously complex treasures, including grape hull pie, jelly, spiced grapes, and homemade wine.

These days, those antique arbors may be sagging or long gone, but the native southern slip-skin grapes themselves, *Vitis rotundiflora*, are making a comeback. Both deep-purple muscadines and green to golden scuppernongs have an increasing presence at farmers' markets and supermarkets. You can also find them in restaurants wherever chefs and southerners are returning to the old ways of eating seasonally, taking time, and valuing flavor over convenience. Both kinds of grapes are members of the muscadine family and are perhaps named for their muscatlike fragrance and sweetness. Scuppernongs get their name from the Scuppernong River in North Carolina's coastal plain. While still a treasure to seek out in the southern wilds, these native grapes have been domesticated and are widely available throughout the region during the late summer and early fall.

Long-treasured and cultivated by Native Americans, these thick-skinned, sweet, and juicy grapes still grow on the edges of the woods and in well-drained bottomlands from Florida to Maryland, and from West Virginia to Texas. Unlike the classic wine-producing grapes of Europe, *Vitis vinifera*, muscadines grow and ripen individually, and are naturally resistant to the devastating disease *phylloxera*. Roanoke Island on North Carolina's Outer Banks is home to the Mother Vine, an enormous muscadine vine believed to be more than 400 years old.

Muscadine wines have been produced in the South since the sixteenth century, and the grapes have long inspired home cooks and culinary entrepreneurs to produce jams, jellies, juice, and more. Eating them out of hand is an earthy delight, given that their skins are extremely thick and their delicious pulp is studded with big seeds. Most people eat the pulp while disposing of the seeds, but some enjoy eating the whole thing. These hardy beauties love the southern summer heat and can take a bit of winter, though not much below 15°.

Muscadine Grape Hull Pie

What a brilliant dish, created by long-ago home cooks who valued thrift, had a creative attitude toward their found ingredients, and noticed that flavor and pleasure await us in unlikely places. Native grapes of the South come encased in sturdy hulls that are very thick and tough when raw. Once they are cooked in a sweet syrup, they become as tender as cherries. This old-school recipe uses everything but the big round seeds. Pies made with deep blue muscadine grapes will give you a gorgeously purple syrup, while pies made with scuppernongs sport a golden hue like juicy apple pies. Wild grape season is short, so make this pie—replete with precious heirloom native fruit—often, during the brief early fall season.

MAKES ONE 9-INCH PIE

Pastry for a 9-inch double-crust pie (page 38)

3/4 cup sugar

1/4 cup all-purpose flour

1/2 teaspoon salt

5 cups muscadine or scuppernong grapes
(about 3 pounds), rinsed

3 tablespoons water

1 tablespoon fresh lemon juice

3 tablespoons cold butter, cut into small pieces

Heat the oven to 400°. Line a 9-inch pie pan with one of the rolled-out piecrusts, leaving a 1-inch overhang. In a small bowl, combine the sugar, flour, and salt and stir with a fork to mix well; set aside.

Squeeze the pulp and seeds from the grapes into a medium saucepan and place the hulls (skins) in a medium bowl. Add the water to the saucepan and bring the pulp to a gentle boil over medium heat; cook until softened and shiny, about 5 minutes. Transfer the pulp to a strainer and place it over the bowl of grape hulls. Using your hands, separate the seeds from the pulp. Discard the seeds and transfer the hulls, juice, and pulp back to the saucepan. Cook over medium heat for 5 minutes more.

Add the sugar mixture and lemon juice to the grapes and stir to mix well. Pour the filling into the piecrust. Sprinkle the small bits of butter evenly over the grape filling. Wet the rim of the bottom piecrust, to help seal it to the top crust.

Cover the filling with the second rolled-out piecrust. Trim away the extra pastry extending beyond the edge of the piecrust already in the pie pan. Gently press the piecrust so that it fits smoothly and evenly over the fruit. Press the edges together to seal them well. Roll the bottom crust edge up and over the top edge and press firmly. Crimp this sealed edge or press it down with the tines of a fork, working your way around the edge of the pie to seal the crust decoratively and well. Use a sharp knife to cut 8 slits in the top crust to allow steam to escape and fruit juices to bubble up as the pie cooks.

Place the pie on a baking sheet to catch drips, and place it on the bottom shelf of the 400° oven and bake for 10 minutes. Reduce the temperature to 350° and bake until the crust is a handsome, golden brown and the grape juices are bubbling up through the crust, 35–40 minutes more. Place the pie on a cooling rack or a folded kitchen towel and let cool for 10 minutes. Serve warm or at room temperature.

Letha Henderson's
Scuppernong Meringue Pie

Growing up by the White Oak River along the North Carolina coast near Swansboro, Letha Henderson learned early on to plant, catch, and gather whatever goodness nature provided. This included both muscadine and scuppernong grapes. Onslow County soil was kind to farm families like hers, who planted corn, sugarcane, vegetables, and feed for dairy cows. This native grape pie takes a little more time to make compared to grape hull pie because the fruit must be processed and then cooked into the luscious custard and finally crowned with meringue. It is worth every minute and every move!

MAKES ONE 9-INCH PIE

Pastry for a 9-inch single-crust pie (page 38)

FOR THE FILLING
1 quart scuppernong or muscadine grapes (4 cups)
1 cup sugar
1 cup heavy cream or half-and-half
3 large egg yolks
1 tablespoon cornstarch

FOR THE MERINGUE
3 large egg whites
6 tablespoons sugar

Heat the oven to 325°. Set out 2 medium saucepans for cooking the scuppernong grape skins and the grape pulp. Line a 9-inch pie pan with the rolled-out piecrust, then crimp the edges decoratively. Refrigerate it until needed.

Wash the grapes and then squeeze the pulp out of the skins into one of the saucepans. Place the grape skins in the other and add 2 tablespoons of water to each pan. Cook both the skins and the pulp over medium heat until each is tender and softened, about 15 minutes. Set the pan of grape skins aside, off the heat. Transfer the grape pulp to a large bowl. When cool enough to handle it easily, squeeze the pulp to extract all the large seeds, discarding them and leaving the grape pulp in the bowl. Mash the grape skins using a potato masher or a fork to break them up a bit. Add the mashed grape skins to the grape pulp.

Add the sugar, heavy cream or half-and-half, egg yolks, and cornstarch to the bowl of grapes and grape skins. Using a fork or a whisk, stir to combine everything evenly and well. Pour the filling into the piecrust.

Place the pie on the bottom shelf of the oven and bake at 325° until the pie is puffy and set, about 45 minutes. Remove the pie from the oven to a cooling rack or a folded kitchen towel to cool while you make the meringue. Increase the oven temperature to 350°.

To make the meringue, in a large bowl, beat the egg whites with an electric mixer on medium speed until foamy. Increase the speed to high and beat until the egg whites thicken to the texture of cream. Add the sugar, 2 tablespoons at a time, beating well after each addition, until the meringue is thick, shiny, and able to hold firm curly peaks.

Scoop the meringue onto the filling, mounding it high in the center and spreading it out to meet the crust, leaving no gaps between meringue and crust. Use the back of a spoon to swirl it into curly shapes.

Place the pie on the middle rack of the oven and bake at 350° until the meringue is handsomely browned, 8–10 minutes.

Place the pie on a cooling rack or a folded kitchen towel and let cool to room temperature.

From *Coastal Carolina Cooking* by Nancy Davis and Kathy Hart. Copyright © 1986 by permission of the University of North Carolina Press. Used by permission of the publisher. www.uncpress.unc.edu

Savory Spiced Muscadine Grapes

Make this classic southern relish as soon as muscadines and scuppernongs appear at fruit stands, farmers' markets, and grocery stores, and don't stop until they run plumb out. Spiced grapes pair handsomely with grilled chicken, sausages, and shellfish, and make a delicious accompaniment to roast chicken or turkey, leg of lamb, pan-fried pork chops, or wild game. Spread this piquant autumnal relish on sandwiches or serve it as an accent to vegan meals, from root vegetable tagines to lentil stew.

MAKES ABOUT 6 HALF-PINT JARS

---

4 pounds muscadine or scuppernong grapes

1 cup water

3½ cups sugar

1½ cups apple cider vinegar or white wine vinegar

1 stick cinnamon

10 whole cloves

1 teaspoon grated mace or grated nutmeg

½ teaspoon salt

Prepare 6 half-pint jars as directed on page 26. Squeeze the grape pulp into a large saucepan and toss the hulls into a large bowl. Place the saucepan over medium-high heat and add the water. Bring to a gentle boil and simmer the pulp for 5 minutes to soften it and release the seeds. Remove from the heat and let cool until easy to handle. Using your hands, squeeze out the seeds, returning the juicy pulp to the saucepan. Discard the seeds and add the grape hulls to the saucepan.

Add the sugar, vinegar, cinnamon, cloves, mace or nutmeg, and salt and stir to mix everything well. Bring to a lively boil over medium-high heat, stirring often to dissolve the sugar and mix in the spices. Reduce the heat to maintain an active simmer. Cook, stirring often, until the mixture is thick and fragrant, 15–20 minutes. Transfer the mixture to a food processor and pulse on and off just to break up the pulp and grape hulls into a pleasing, chunky relish with a coarse texture. Return to the saucepan and let cool. Transfer the spiced grapes to the prepared jars. Cover tightly and refrigerate for up to 3 weeks.

Sandra Gutierrez's Drunken Chicken with Muscadine Grapes and White Wine

My friend Sandra Gutierrez illuminates the numerous and distinctive cuisines of Latin America in her cookbooks, blog posts, feature stories, and cooking classes. Her deep personal knowledge and extensive research make her an extraordinary guide to the ingredients, flavors, recipes, and traditions of the Spanish-speaking world. In this dish from her groundbreaking book The New Southern-Latino Table, *Sandra notes that in numerous Latin American countries chicken stewed with wine, including the* estofados *of Panama and the fricassees of Cuba, is a popular dish. For this dish, she found inspiration in cooking of Chile, Latin America's wine country, where oregano is a beloved herb. She notes that a Chilean Chardonnay would make an especially fine ingredient in this lovely dish.*

MAKES 6 SERVINGS

1 large chicken (4½ to 5 pounds), cut into 10 serving pieces
1½ teaspoons salt
½ teaspoon freshly ground black or white pepper
2 tablespoons extra-virgin olive oil
5 cups thinly sliced Vidalia onion
3 large garlic cloves, thinly sliced
2 tablespoons Dijon mustard
1 bay leaf
½ teaspoon red pepper flakes
1 cup dry white wine
3 cups muscadine or scuppernong grapes, halved and seeded (see Note)
A handful of finely chopped fresh parsley

Pat the chicken dry with paper towels, and season with the salt and pepper. In a large Dutch oven, heat the oil over medium-high heat. Working in batches, brown the chicken pieces on all sides, and transfer them to a platter. Discard all but one tablespoon of the oil remaining in the pan.

Add the onions to the pan and cook over medium heat, stirring occasionally, until they are soft and shiny, 4–5 minutes. Add the garlic, mustard, bay leaf, and red pepper flakes, and cook, stirring often, until the garlic is fragrant, about 30 seconds. Add the wine and deglaze by scraping the bottom of the pan, letting the wine come to a boil. Return the chicken to the pan, along with all the juices that have collected at the bottom of the platter. Cover, reduce the heat to low, and simmer for 15 minutes.

Add the halved, seeded grapes, and stir well. Cover and simmer until the chicken is cooked through and the juices run clear when the chicken is pierced with a fork, about 25 minutes. Taste the sauce and adjust with salt and pepper as needed. Transfer the stew to a deep serving platter or large serving bowl, sprinkle with parsley, and serve hot.

NOTE ❋ If any skins slip off the grapes as you prepare them, include those skins in the recipe, as they bring flavor and texture to the finished dish.

You can substitute another grape variety, removing the seeds if necessary. Cook the sauce for 10–12 minutes longer to reduce it, since only muscadines and scuppernongs contain extra pectin, which helps to thicken the sauce.

Pawpaws

Pawpaws ought to be famous. They're huge, they're an American original, they're sweet, delicious, and nutritious, and they're free for the gathering each autumn in twenty-six states. Pawpaws (*Asimina triloba*) are the largest-sized indigenous fruit in the country, growing in kooky clusters from tropical trees that have thrived since prehistoric times in the temperate forests of the eastern United States. Their sweet, golden, and custardy fruit tastes like a wild mash-up of bananas, pineapple, and mangoes, serving up protein and vitamin C, along with sweetness and sustenance. Their huge oval leaves turn sunflower-golden in autumn, and the trees provide habitat for the zebra swallowtail butterfly.

Despite its girth and goodness, the humble pawpaw remains largely unknown, the mysterious star of the childhood ditty, "picking up pawpaws, put 'em in your pocket." We tend to know the song but not its subject. Pawpaw's problem is counterintuitive. These bulbous green fruits look sturdy but are easily bruised and crushed when ripe. Their delicate nature and brief shelf life makes them poor candidates for shipping and storing, two essential features for commercial success in the food business, past as well as present.

Native Americans knew pawpaws' value and pleasures and cultivated them long before contact with European explorers. Their botanical name, *Asimina*, comes from their Algonquin-language name, *assimin* or *rassimin*. This ubiquitous wild fruit proved essential to members of the Lewis and Clark expedition and served as sustenance for African Americans escaping slavery through the forested routes of the Underground Railroad. Given the numerous lakes, roads, creeks, and towns named after the pawpaw, it's clear that the fruit has long been known and appreciated in local communities, where its fragile nature posed no transportation problems.

Thanks to the dedicated and diligent work on the part of pawpaw enthusiasts in the fields of agriculture and culinary arts, pawpaws have become the subject of interest and experimentation. Neal Peterson, known affectionately as Johnny Pawpawseed for his decades of advocacy, has led the way, as have the research-centered activities of Kentucky State University and many other institutions. Increasingly pawpaws are known, loved, and sought out by home gardeners, proponents of organic agriculture, advocates of sustainability, cooks, and chefs. This relative of the tropical cherimoya, custard apple, and soursop shines as a fruit to enjoy out of hand and as an ingredient in ice cream, smoothies, cookies, and breads.

To check ripeness on a green pawpaw, press gently with your thumb near the stem, as you would test an avocado or a peach. If it gives easily, it's ready to eat. Do so within 2 or 3 days, because pawpaws move swiftly from perfect readiness to overripe.

To eat, slice a pawpaw in half and spoon out its sweet, custardy goodness on the spot. Or scoop it out of its skin into a bowl and use a spoon to remove its big brown seeds. The fruit freezes well. To freeze after separating it from the peel, either purée the fruit or leave it whole. Whole or puréed, transfer the fruit to an airtight container, press plastic wrap on the surface to preserve its color from oxidation, cover, and freeze for up to 6 months.

Pawpaw Custard Pie

A traditional southern-style egg custard pie makes an excellent showcase for the rich, fruity, and delicate flavor of pawpaws. Stirred into the eggs, milk, and sugar composing a classic custard, the fruit's wild sweetness comes through nicely. This pie is best within a day of making it, and the top portion of the custard may darken a little, giving it a pleasing two-tone effect.

MAKES ONE 9-INCH PIE

Pastry for a 9-inch single-crust pie (page 38)
1¼ cups whole milk
4 large eggs
¾ cups sugar
1 teaspoon pure vanilla extract
¼ teaspoon salt
1 cup pawpaw purée

Heat the oven to 375°. Line a 9-inch pie pan with the rolled-out piecrust and then line the piecrust with a large piece of parchment or waxed paper. Fill the piecrust with dried beans, uncooked rice, or pie weights. Bake for 10 minutes. Carefully remove the parchment paper and its contents. (Cool and store the beans, rice, or pie weights in a resealable plastic bag for future piecrusts). Return the piecrust to the oven and bake for 5 more minutes, or until the surface of the crust is a little puffy and dry but still underbaked. Remove the piecrust from the oven and set it aside while you prepare the filling.

Reduce the oven temperature to 350°.

In a medium saucepan, bring the milk almost to a boil over medium heat. The milk should be steaming hot, fragrant, and forming tiny bubbles around the edge of the pan. Remove from the heat and set aside.

In a medium bowl, beat the eggs with a whisk or a fork until they are very well combined. Add the sugar, vanilla, and salt and whisk well to dissolve the sugar. Slowly add the warm milk, whisking constantly but gently, until it is well incorporated. Add the pawpaw purée and stir well to combine everything into a smooth custard.

Pour the filling into the piecrust and bake at 350° for 35–45 minutes, or until the custard is smooth and set and the crust is nicely browned. Though the custard should be firm, a little jiggling at the center is fine. Transfer the pie to a cooling rack or a folded kitchen town and cool. Serve at room temperature. Store the pie in the refrigerator, covered with plastic wrap or foil, for up to 2 days.

HOW TO PREPARE PAWPAWS FOR EATING, COOKING, AND STORING

Cut a ripe pawpaw in half lengthwise. Gently twist the fruit apart as you would an avocado, moving the halves in opposite directions. Use a large spoon to scoop the pulp out into bowl. Remove the seeds using your hands or a spoon.

You can leave the fruit in natural chunks or chop it up. For many recipes, you will need the fruit mashed or puréed. You can mash it by hand with a potato masher. For a smooth, even-textured purée, use a blender or food processor. Use in recipes as you would use pumpkin, applesauce, or mashed bananas.

To store or freeze, transfer the pulp, in chunks, mashed, or puréed, to an airtight container. Press plastic wrap or waxed paper on the surface of the fruit to keep air away from it. Alternatively, spoon it into resealable freezer storage bags, pressing out as much air as possible before closing them. Store in the refrigerator for up to 3 days or freeze for up to 6 months.

Pawpaw Ice Cream

The ideal way to taste the sweetly earthy and unique flavor of pawpaw is in uncooked dishes, such as puddings, smoothies, and ice cream. Here is a cool and luscious way to enjoy this underappreciated national treasure. You can make it during pawpaw season, when the fruits are abundantly available at farmers' markets, or use frozen pawpaw purée, which retains its flavor wonderfully to enjoy year-round.

MAKES ABOUT 1 QUART

3/4 cup milk

2/3 cup sugar

1/4 teaspoon salt

1 1/2 cups heavy cream

1 teaspoon pure vanilla extract

1 cup pawpaw purée

Combine the milk, sugar, salt, cream, and vanilla in a large bowl. Use a whisk or a large spoon to stir well until the sugar dissolves and everything is evenly combined. Stir in the pawpaw purée and mix well. Cover and chill for at least 3 hours or overnight.

Transfer the pawpaw mixture to an ice cream maker and freeze according to the manufacturer's directions. For firm texture, transfer the ice cream to a covered container and freeze for at least 2 hours. Set it out for about 15 minutes before serving to soften for easy scooping.

Pawpaw Caramel Sauce

This luscious dessert sauce pairs the wild, sweet flavor of paw-paws with the toasty goodness of caramel. It makes a fine flourish spooned over vanilla ice cream, drizzled on pound cake, or spooned over a warm bowl of bread pudding. It keeps well in the refrigerator for two weeks. Serve at room temperature or warm it gently before serving.

MAKES 1 CUP

1½ cups sugar

⅔ cup water

1 tablespoon light or dark corn syrup

¾ cup heavy cream

¾ cup pawpaw purée

In a heavy medium saucepan, combine the sugar, water, and corn syrup. Stir well and then bring to a lively boil over medium-high heat. Stir well and continue cooking, without stirring, for 5–7 minutes, or until the mixture begins to darken and becomes a warm, handsome golden brown.

Remove the pan from the heat. Slowly pour in the cream — the hot syrup will boil up, sizzle, and steam noisily for a few moments. Stir well using a whisk or a large spoon. Return the pan to the stove and cook, stirring often, to warm the caramel sauce completely.

Transfer the sauce to a medium bowl. Add the pawpaw purée and stir to mix it into the caramel sauce completely. Cool the sauce to room temperature and then transfer it to a covered jar. Store in the refrigerator for up to 2 weeks.

Pawpaw Yogurt Smoothie

While native to the forests of the eastern United States, pawpaws look like tropical fruits with their brightness in color and flavor. With their resemblance to mangoes in color and texture, pawpaws make a delightfully colored yogurt-based smoothie. You can make this refreshing and satisfying beverage using fresh pawpaws or frozen pawpaw purée.

MAKES 2–3 SERVINGS

1 cup pawpaw purée

¼ cup water

1 cup plain yogurt

4 ice cubes

2 tablespoons brown sugar, lightly packed

1 tablespoon fresh lime juice or lemon juice

In the jar of a blender, combine the pawpaw purée, water, yogurt, ice cubes, brown sugar, and lime or lemon juice. Blend for 30 seconds and then stop and scrape down the sides of the blender jar. Continue processing 1–2 minutes more, pulsing the blender to bring everything together evenly and well, until you have a thick, rich smoothie. Transfer to tall glasses and serve at once.

Peaches

Summertime road trips home from North Carolina's Kure Beach used to take us along two-lane highways through small towns with rows of fruit stands offering peaches by the bushel. We would stop to quench our thirst on Nehi's with nabs and pick out a big basket of peaches to carry home. Emblematic of sun-drenched summertime sweetness, peaches from the sand hills of North Carolina eaten out of hand provided sticky, juicy relief from the sultry heat. My mother took half of them to our grandparents' dairy farm, where my grandmother steamed up the kitchen making peach jam for biscuits and pickled peaches for holiday meals, the kind with a tablecloth in the dining room and moderate misbehavior at the kids' table in the kitchen.

Back then I knew nothing about southern peach culture—that Georgia was the Peach State and that South Carolina had crowned the blushing fuzzy orbs as their state fruit. Our family dinner table often featured store-bought canned peaches, and while I liked them, I didn't make the connection between the slick, syrupy golden crescents in my bowl and the sun-warmed juice bombs we had devoured just a few months earlier halfway home from the beach.

Nowadays, I'm a peach devotee, enchanted by their beautiful shape, color, and texture, appreciative of the beauty of peach trees, from first blossom, to leafed out with emerald-green C-shaped leaves, to decorated with tempting fruit. When we moved from Southern

California to my home state of North Carolina more than a decade ago, I blithely planted a peach tree in our heavily shaded backyard. It obliged, surviving the winter and popping out a half a dozen small, greenish, rock-hard peaches, which I watched eagerly and with pride, though I had done very little on their behalf. Then I noticed their numbers dwindling, and as their numbers plummeted, I checked from the back porch and saw a squirrel holding the last small peach between his tiny paws, chomping away at a leisurely, confident pace. The tree seemed to lose steam just as I did, perhaps because these universally adored stone fruits need sun, food, and attention from a knowledgeable gardener.

Prunus persica traces its roots back to the Yangtze River valley in China, where its ancestors were domesticated and cultivated some 5,000 years ago. Because of ancient Persia's appreciation for the stone fruit, it has received the Latin name meaning "Persian plum." Peaches share the *Prunus* genus with many stone fruits, including apricots, cherries, and plums, as well as almonds and nectarines.

Peach aficionados introduced the fruit to Greece and Rome, and from there peaches found favor throughout Europe. Spanish explorers planted peach trees in Florida in the 1500s, and although the explorers departed, Native Americans continued to cultivate peaches, spreading peach culture northward over time. When William Penn and other new arrivals to the New World encountered these cultivated peaches growing in Pennsylvania and Virginia, they wrongly assumed that they were an indigenous species of peach. Both George Washington and Thomas Jefferson grew peach trees in their respective orchards, and while much of the fruit was eaten out of hand and in pastry, or put up as jams, preserves, and compotes, an enormous amount was made into cider and brandy, also known as mobby.

Peaches are not the easiest fruit tree to grow, being prone to disease, sensitive to frosts around blossoming time, and requiring some 500 hours of chilling at temperatures between 32° and 50°. Despite these challenges, commercial peach production was under way in Maryland, Delaware, Georgia, and Virginia by the nineteenth century, and peach orchards were a feature of many a homestead in areas where the weather allowed the trees to thrive.

In *The Carolina Housewife*, published in 1847, Sarah Rutledge included recipes for peach sherbet, peach preserves, dried peaches, pickled peaches, peach marmalade, and peach leather. Edna Lewis, in *The Taste of Country Cooking*, her luminous memoir about growing up in rural Freetown, Virginia, in the 1920s, shares recipes for brandied peaches, peach cobbler with a lattice top and freshly grated nutmeg sauce, crushed peaches, and peach ice cream. In *Dori Sanders's Country Cooking: Recipes and Stories from our Family Farmstand*, Miss Sanders talks about growing up on her family's peach farm in Filbert, South Carolina, providing recipes for peaches and much more, and sharing a portrait of how we can maintains traditions and old-time flavors in the twenty-first century.

Though modern agricultural efforts have gone toward making peaches firmer, redder, less fuzzy, and sturdier for shipping, many old-time varieties remain. Keep your eye out for some worthy peaches next time summer comes around, and make this 5,000-year-old round and fuzzy treasure a part of your kitchen routines.

Fresh Peach Chutney

I love the sunny color and piquant flavors of this British-style chutney. It pairs wonderfully with roast chicken, spicy shrimp curry, rice pilaf, or anything sizzling-hot off the grill.

MAKES 3 CUPS

3 cups coarsely chopped ripe peaches
1 cup coarsely chopped apple
1 cup finely chopped onion
$\frac{1}{2}$ cup finely chopped bell pepper, any color
$\frac{1}{2}$ cup raisins
$\frac{1}{4}$ cup chopped candied ginger (optional)
$\frac{1}{2}$ cup sugar
$\frac{1}{2}$ cup apple cider vinegar or white vinegar
$1\frac{1}{2}$ teaspoons mustard seeds
1 teaspoon red pepper flakes
$\frac{1}{2}$ teaspoon salt

In a 3-quart saucepan or Dutch oven, combine the peaches, apples, onions, and bell peppers. Stir with a large spoon to mix them well. Add the raisins, candied ginger, if using, sugar, vinegar, mustard seeds, red pepper flakes, and salt and stir well. Bring to a lively boil over medium-high heat. Stir to coat all the ingredients evenly.

Adjust the heat to maintain a gentle but active simmer. Cook, stirring now and then, until the chutney has thickened a little, formed a pleasing syrup, and developed its flavor, 30–40 minutes. Remove from the heat and let cool to room temperature. Serve at room temperature. Cover and store in the refrigerator for up to 2–3 weeks.

HOW TO PEEL FRESH PEACHES

Blanching peaches makes peeling easy without sacrificing any of the deliciousness beneath the peel. To blanch peaches, bring a medium saucepan of water to a rolling boil over high heat. Meanwhile, place a medium bowl filled with cold water next to the stove.

When the water is boiling rapidly, gently lower two or three peaches at a time into the water and cook for 30–60 seconds. Using a large, heatproof slotted spoon, transfer them to the cold water. Repeat with the remaining peaches.

Using a sharp paring knife, gently slice into the stem end of each peach, just enough to lift up the peel. Pull the skin away from the fruit, following the curve of the peach, and discard the skin. Continue until the peach is peeled completely.

Bill Smith's Green Peach Salad

This wonderful and useful recipe comes from Bill Smith, the brilliant and beloved chef at Crook's Corner in Chapel Hill, North Carolina. Bill writes cookbooks and food stories and teaches cooking classes. His generosity, creativity, smarts, and kindness have earned him more fans than there are peaches in South Carolina and Georgia put together. This brilliant recipe gives us a way to appreciate and enjoy peaches that are a little ahead of their time. Turning tender but not yet ripe and sweet, they work wonderfully in this piquant and refreshing salad. How quintessentially Bill Smith, to see the possibilities in something everybody else wrote off. Plan to make this within a few hours of serving time, as it does not keep well.

MAKES 4–6 SERVINGS

2½ pounds unripe peaches, peeled, pitted, and
    sliced into wedges as for a pie
Scant ½ cup sugar
½ teaspoon salt
2 tablespoons fresh mint leaves
3 tablespoons freshly ground black or white pepper
2 tablespoons extra-virgin olive oil, preferably a flavorful one

---

In a medium bowl, toss the peaches with the sugar and salt. Let them sit for 10 minutes. Meanwhile, stack the mint leaves up in little piles and cut them crosswise into long, slender strips. Set aside until the peaches and sugar have become shiny and given off a little syrup. Add the pepper, olive oil, and mint leaves and stir to mix them well. Cover and chill until serving time. Serve cold or at cool room temperature.

Peach Custard Pie with a Secret

This traditional southern confection is a pie with a secret. What looks like a lovely egg custard pie conceals a delicious jammy layer of sweet peaches. Because of this contrast between what seems to be and what is, the pie is also known as hypocrite pie. This negativity seemed unworthy of this lovely antique dish, so I came up with a new name that salutes the mystery. Originally made with dried peaches or apples, it must have been a delightful treat during wintertime, when peaches basking in dazzling sunshine were a distant memory. Try this pie with blackberries, strawberries, or apples in place of the peaches, simmering the fruit with sugar first in order to create a glossy richness.

MAKES ONE 9-INCH PIE

Pastry for a 9-inch single-crust pie (page 38)

FOR THE FILLING
2 cups peeled, coarsely chopped peaches
$\frac{1}{4}$ cup sugar
1 tablespoon fresh lemon juice
Pinch of salt

FOR THE CUSTARD
3 large eggs
$1\frac{1}{4}$ cups milk
$\frac{1}{2}$ cup sugar
1 teaspoon pure vanilla extract

Heat the oven to 350°. Line a 9-inch pie pan with the rolled-out piecrust.

To make the filling, combine the peaches, sugar, lemon juice, and salt in a medium saucepan. Cook over medium-high heat until the sugar dissolves and the peach juices form a syrup, 2–3 minutes. Reduce the heat and simmer, stirring often, until the peaches are tender and surrounded by sauce, 10–15 minutes. Transfer the peach mixture to a bowl to cool.

To make the custard, in a medium bowl, combine the eggs, milk, sugar, and vanilla. Use a whisk or a fork to beat this mixture well, dissolving the sugar and combining the eggs and milk into a smooth custard.

Spread the peaches over the piecrust in an even layer. Carefully pour the custard over the peaches. If some of the peaches float, gently press them down and try to keep them hidden from view. Bake at 350° until the custard has puffed and is set all over, 40–50 minutes. Place the pie on a cooling rack or a folded kitchen towel to cool. Serve at room temperature.

Fresh Peach Fritters

Peach fritters have been one of the stars of southern cooking since colonial times. They were made year-round, since preserved peaches could be used during the winter months. A simple batter, quickly stirred together and studded with chunks of peach, fries up in minutes, yielding puffy golden orbs of sweet goodness. I love to make small ones, because they cook quickly and evenly and have a handsome, crisp exterior that enhances their flavor.

MAKES ABOUT 24 SMALL FRITTERS

---

2 large eggs

$\frac{1}{2}$ cup milk

$1\frac{1}{2}$ cups all-purpose flour

3 tablespoons sugar

1 teaspoon baking powder

$\frac{1}{2}$ teaspoon salt

$\frac{1}{4}$ teaspoon grated nutmeg

1 tablespoon melted butter

2–3 medium peaches, peeled and chopped into
    $\frac{1}{2}$-inch pieces (about $1\frac{1}{2}$ cups)

Vegetable oil for deep-frying

Confectioner's sugar for sprinkling on hot fritters

In a small bowl, stir the eggs and milk with a fork to mix them evenly and well. In a medium bowl, combine the flour, sugar, baking powder, salt, and nutmeg and stir with a whisk or a fork to mix well. Add the milk/egg mixture to the dry ingredients and stir just until combined, making a thick batter. Add the peaches and stir gently with a big spoon or a spatula to mix them in evenly.

To cook the fritters, have the following near the stove: a wire cooling rack covered with paper towels on a baking sheet to absorb some of the oil from the fritters after frying; a slotted spoon or a large wire skimmer for scooping the cooked fritters out of the oil quickly when they are done; 2 soup spoons, cereal spoons, or teaspoons to use in forming the fritters.

Pour the vegetable oil into a medium Dutch oven or a large, deep skillet to a depth of 3 inches. Heat the oil over medium-high heat until it registers 375° on a candy/deep-fry thermometer, or until a drop of batter sinks and then floats to the top at once. Using the 2 spoons, scoop up about a tablespoon of the batter and very carefully scrape it into the bubbling oil. Continue until you have 5–7 fritters bobbing in the hot oil. Cook the fritters, turning once or twice to help them cook evenly, until they are puffed up and golden brown, 2–3 minutes (see Note). Check for doneness by cutting a plump one open. The center should not be gooey. If the center is cooked through, scoop the fritters up quickly, holding them over the pot for a few seconds to drain well, and transfer them to the prepared rack. Let the fritters cool for a minute or two, transfer them to a serving platter, and shower them with confectioners' sugar. Serve hot or warm.

NOTE ❋ If the fritters brown too quickly, they will be perfectly done outside but have raw batter inside. Adjust the temperature as you cook, so that they cook swiftly but evenly, inside and out. Cut open a fritter now and then to check the inside for doneness.

If you enjoy deep-frying, consider purchasing an electric deep-fryer. The fryer keeps the oil temperature constant, simplifying the process.

Surry County Peach Sonker with Dip

"Sonker" is a particular word for a particular traditional dessert in a particular place. The place is Surry County, North Carolina, located between Winston-Salem, North Carolina, and the Virginia border. The dessert is what I grew up calling a cobbler, made with piecrust dough lining the pan and on the top. This cobbler is baked in a large, deep rectangular pan rather than a pie plate. Its standard companion is a luscious milk sauce that's poured over each serving while still warm. This "dip" involves no dipping, and no one can explain the origins of the term "sonker." Therefore, let us dwell in the sweet mystery, pondering the possibilities while preparing and baking this classic southern fruit recipe.

MAKES ONE 13 × 9-INCH SONKER

FOR THE PIE

Pastry for three 9-inch single-crust pies (page 38)

1½ cups sugar

⅓ cup all-purpose flour

1½ teaspoons ground cinnamon

1 teaspoon ground nutmeg

½ teaspoon salt

3½ pounds fresh peaches, peeled and cut into large chunks (about 9 cups), or 9 cups frozen peeled peaches cut into chunks

½ cup (1 stick) butter, melted

½ cup water

FOR THE DIP

½ cup sugar

3 tablespoons cornstarch

3 cups milk

½ teaspoon pure vanilla extract

For the piecrust, drape one of the three rolled-out circles of pastry dough over half of a 13 × 9-inch baking pan and carefully press the dough up the sides and into the corners of the pan. Trim away the excess dough, leaving 1 inch of overhang, and use it, along with a second rolled-out circle of dough, to piece and patch together the rest of the lining for the pan, being sure to extend the edges of the dough 1 inch beyond the rim. Gently press the dough to seal up any seams.

Cut the remaining rolled-out circle of pastry dough into 1-inch-wide strips. To make a crisscross pattern on top of the sonker, you will need six 14-inch-long strips and twelve 10-inch-long strips. Don't worry about perfection—you can piece together strips of dough as you go along to get enough strips to arrange over the fruit filling. Set the pastry-lined pan and dough strips aside while you prepare the filling. (You may have some extra dough. If so, simply wrap it airtight and place in the freezer for another use.)

Heat the oven to 450°. In a large bowl, combine the sugar, flour, cinnamon, nutmeg, and salt. Use a fork to stir everything together well. Add the peaches and gently stir and toss until the fruit is evenly coated with the sugar mixture.

Pour the filling into the pan and spread it out into an even layer. Pour the butter and then the water evenly over the peaches. Carefully arrange the six longer pastry strips lengthwise on top of the peach filling, placing them evenly spaced so that the filling shows through. Arrange the twelve shorter pastry strips crosswise over the long strips. Press the end of each pastry strip firmly against the sides of the pan so that it sticks to the crust. Fold the top edge of the pastry down and over the sealed strips and press it against the pastry-lined sides of the pan, going all the way around the rim of the pan. Crimp this crust edge by pinching it into little points, or press it with the tines of a fork to make a design.

Place the sonker on the middle shelf of the oven and bake for 10 minutes. Lower the heat to 350° and bake until the crust is handsomely and evenly browned and the filling is bubbling up vigorously, 45–55 minutes more. Place the sonker on a cooling rack or a folded kitchen towel and let cool for 10 minutes.

While the sonker bakes, make the dip. In a small or medium saucepan, combine the sugar and cornstarch and stir with a fork to mix well. Add the milk and vanilla, and stir to dissolve the sugar mixture into the milk. Place the saucepan over medium-high heat and stir as the mixture comes to a boil. As soon as it boils, reduce the heat so that it maintains a lively simmer, and cook, stirring often, until it thickens and is smooth, 3–5 minutes. Remove from the heat and set aside to cool.

Serve the sonker warm or at room temperature, passing the dip in a pitcher or in a small bowl with a spoon for serving.

Persimmons

Like tiny deflating balloons, forlorn and abandoned after a celebration in the autumn outdoors, ripe wild persimmons seem more like candidates for compost than a culinary treasure. Yet as any fan of old-school persimmon pudding will tell you, kitchen gold is exactly what they are. A challenge to locate and a mess to process, wild persimmons are like a handwritten letters from another place and time, unique in flavor and texture, worth the effort they require, and an enduring source of inspiration for cold-weather cooks.

If you're looking to find a wild persimmon tree, my home state of North Carolina is a fine place to start. From the Blue Ridge and Great Smoky Mountains to the rural byways down east, *Diospyros virginiana* flourishes, wild and free. Along the perimeter of cultivated fields, railroad tracks, and country roads, they love living on the edge, soaring upwards of seventy feet in height. One of the last trees to leaf out in the spring, persimmon trees flower in early summer and drop their plump, ping-pong-ball-sized, pumpkin-hued fruit from September through the end of the year.

Southern they may be, but persimmons, much like apples and pears, don't know borders. They grow happily from New York down to Florida, and from the Atlantic coastline to the Midwest. Heartland states, including Indiana, Missouri, Iowa, and Ohio, all have an abundance of persimmon trees, and what we think of as the quintessential southern pudding-friend, the fruit varies only slightly throughout the enormous range of persimmon-growing locales.

Native Americans valued the tree for its multiple benefits, employing both its bark and fruit in traditional medicines and remedies. They enjoyed the ripe fruit out of hand but also transformed it into beverages, puddings, and porridge and dried the pulp for wintertime nourishment and enjoyment. Colonial settlers benefited greatly from Native Americans' knowledge of the tree, especially during the difficult winters early in the colonial era. The English name persimmon comes from the Powatan/Algonquin word for the plush, worthy fruit: *putchamin*. The species name *virginiana* comes from Captain John Smith's Jamestown, Virginia, from where he wrote home to England in the early 1600s praising the precious indigenous fruit.

Persimmons in the wild resemble their cultivated counterparts, Hachiya and Fuyu persimmons, both in color and in their ability to thrive despite cold winter weather, even through snows and frost. Like their Asian cousins, American persimmons can linger on the branches like holiday ornaments long after the deciduous leaves have fallen. You needn't wait for frost or a hard freeze to enjoy them, though, since their ripening time isn't related to freezing temperatures. Waiting until they are fully ripened, however, makes great sense, as anyone who has sampled a green or underripe persimmon will tell you. The astringent, tannic taste of unripe persimmons makes them easy to resist until they signal their state of ripeness by dropping to the ground.

A large persimmon fan club will likely be keeping close watch to determine when the getting is good. Deer, squirrels, possums, raccoons, and birds share humans' appreciation of the luscious autumnal orbs, and since the ripe ones must land and become available at ground level, no creature gets a head start.

To gather persimmons the old-time way, place an old bed sheet, bedspread, blanket, or tarp under a tree full of nearly ripe or ripe persimmons at night, and get out there first thing in the morning so you can collect the precious fruit before other creatures get a crack at it. Ripe persimmons look more like compost material than a cook's delight, but don't be deceived! The faint bluish tinge some display is a sign of sweetness.

For their size, wild persimmons have an abundance of seeds, as many as six in one small orb; this makes the job of obtaining enough pulp to make a pudding a bit of a challenge. Food mills work for many people, but not for me. I set my standard kitchen colander in a large, shallow stainless steel bowl or on a jelly roll pan and press the ripe fruit onto the holes with my hand or a spatula or large spoon. The purée will pass through the good-sized holes, leaving the seeds behind. The skin of wild persimmons is thin and delicate, so much of it is absorbed into the purée as it is pressed through a mill, colander, or sieve.

Whole persimmons keep well, so you can process them for cooking shortly before you need them. The pulp freezes well, too; place two-cup portions (a perfect amount for pudding), in freezer bags, flatten the filled bags to push the air out, and stack them flat in the freezer. If you live in persimmon country, check farmers' markets and local food outlets for frozen persimmon pulp, which is often available during the fall season. A number of farmers' markets here in North Carolina have vendors selling persimmon purée. Persimmon pudding is the classic use for this wild treasure, but consider spreading the goodness around by making persimmon cookies, pies, muffins, and ice cream.

Persimmon Ice Cream

Vegan and super easy to make, this extraordinary ice cream marries the deep rustic flavor of persimmons with the sweet velvety goodness of coconut milk. I love the spices in this recipe, but if you prefer a pure persimmon taste, simply omit the cinnamon, ginger, and nutmeg from the recipe.

MAKES ABOUT 1 PINT

1 cup sugar

1 teaspoon ground cinnamon

$\frac{1}{2}$ teaspoon ground ginger

$\frac{1}{2}$ teaspoon grated nutmeg

$\frac{1}{2}$ teaspoon salt

2 (14-ounce) cans unsweetened coconut milk, divided

$\frac{3}{4}$ cup persimmon purée

In a medium saucepan, combine the sugar, cinnamon, ginger, nutmeg, and salt and stir with a fork to combine them evenly and well. Add one can of the coconut milk to the saucepan and bring to just barely a boil over medium-high heat, stirring often.

Remove from the heat at once and add the remaining coconut milk. Stir well with a large spoon or a whisk until the mixture is very smooth. Set aside to cool for about 15 minutes.

Add the persimmon purée and stir to mix it in evenly and well. Transfer to an airtight container and chill until very cold, at least 4 hours, or overnight. Transfer to an ice cream freezer and freeze according to the manufacturer's instructions.

HOW TO PREPARE WILD PERSIMMONS

Turning wild persimmons into a smooth, luscious, autumn-colored purée makes a considerable mess, but your efforts will be rewarded with a priceless culinary treasure, ready to flavor all kinds of delicious dishes. Frozen in airtight containers, persimmon purée will keep for up to 1 year.

To extract the pulp from wild persimmons, you will need a colander to separate the seeds and caps from the creamy fruit, and a sieve to strain out the remaining bits of woodsy distractions. You will also need several large bowls to hold the fruit and purée as you process it.

Place a colander in a large bowl or roasting pan in which to catch the purée as it is separated from the seeds. Add about 3 cups of whole persimmons to the colander and use your hands to press and stir and push the fruit against the holes, extruding the pulp while leaving the seeds behind. Transfer the seeds to a small bowl and continue adding whole persimmons to the colander until you have separated the seeds from the entire batch. Discard the seeds, skin, and other detritus.

Place a fine-mesh strainer or sieve over another large bowl and add about 3 cups of persimmon pulp to the strainer. Using a spatula, a pestle, a large spoon, or your hands, press, scoop, and rub the persimmon pulp against the bottom of the strainer to separate any additional fibers, skin, stems, and seeds that remain in the pulp. Scrape the outside of the strainer occasionally in order to collect the pulp. When you have extracted the pulp from the first batch, scoop out and discard the seeds, skin, and fibers remaining in the strainer. Add a new batch of whole persimmons and repeat the process. When you have finished straining out all the unwanted portions of the fruit, transfer the pulp to a resealable container; cover and refrigerate for up to 3 days. Or transfer it to airtight containers or freezer-proof plastic bags and freeze for up to 6 months. Consider freezing it in 1- or 2-cup portions so that you can defrost just enough for most recipes.

HOW TO PREPARE DOMESTIC PERSIMMONS

Two types of persimmons, fuyus and hachiyas, are widely available at supermarkets and often at farmers markets during their late-fall through early-winter season. The fuyu resembles a plump, petite tomato, and the hachiya has a broad, rounded top and pointed end. Both belong to the botanical family *Diospyros kaki* and are among the more than 200 species of domesticated persimmons.

Fuyus are quite firm, even when ripe, making them easy to slice for eating. To prepare them for use in recipes, use a paring knife to cut out the stem portion, and then peel off the skin from using a vegetable peeler or paring knife. Cut the fruit lengthwise into wedges. To make purée, halve the fruit crosswise and remove any seeds. Chop the fruit into large chunks and purée in a blender or food processor.

The larger and more delicate hachiyas soften as they ripen. Once ripe, their texture is like that of an overripe mango, too moist to chop or slice. To prepare hachiyas for eating, cut them in half lengthwise and scoop out the pulp into a bowl and remove any seeds. Unlike fuyus, the pulp may not need to be puréed to use in recipes, as it is quite soft when ripe. If underripe, you can purée it as you would a fuyu persimmon. If you want a very smooth texture, press the pulp through a fine-mesh strainer.

Fuyu and hachiya persimmon purée can be kept covered and refrigerated for up to 3 days. Packed in airtight containers or freezer bags, it freezes well for up to 6 months.

Old-Time Persimmon Pudding

Wild persimmons are a precious gift from Mother Nature to southern home cooks, delivered each fall in messy profusion. Sticky and packed with seeds, they demand time and attention, out under the trees and in the kitchen. Why bother, one might ask, if one had never had old-time persimmon pudding, or not loved it as I do. It's a very moist, dense cake, somewhere between fudge and cake in texture and with a taste exactly like the colors of fall. Cultivated persimmons yield a lovely, milder version of this homespun classic dish, and a purée of sweet potatoes or pumpkin works nicely, too. A little whipped cream or heavy cream makes a lovely accompaniment to this dessert.

MAKES ONE 13 × 9-INCH PUDDING

2 cups all-purpose flour

1½ cups sugar

1 teaspoon cinnamon

1 teaspoon baking soda

¼ teaspoon salt

2 cups persimmon pulp (about 2 pounds ripe persimmons)

1¾ cups milk

2 large eggs

4 tablespoons butter, melted

Heat the oven to 350°. Generously grease a 13 × 9-inch pan. Combine the flour, sugar, cinnamon, baking soda, and salt in a medium bowl and use a fork to mix them together very well.

In a large bowl, combine the persimmon pulp, milk, eggs, and butter and stir with a whisk or a fork to mix them together well. Add the flour to the persimmon mixture and stir with a whisk or wooden spoon to mix everything into a smooth batter.

Pour the batter into the prepared pan and bake at 350° for 40–50 minutes, or until the pudding springs back when touched gently in the center and is beginning to pull away from the sides of the pan.

Place the pan on a wire rack or a folded kitchen towel and cool completely. Cut into squares and serve plain or with sweetened whipped cream.

Bill Neal's Elegant Persimmon Pudding

In his signature recipe for this iconic southern dessert, Bill Neal created an ethereal version of this beloved autumn dish. Where the traditional version of persimmon pudding is a moist cake served in squares, sturdy and steadfast like a rocking chair on the porch, Neal's persimmon pudding soars in the pan like a soufflé. Scooped into bowls and garnished with a glorious cloud of sweetened whipped cream, this is a fall favorite at Crook's Corner in Chapel Hill, N.C. It enchants both old-timers and modern diners with its familiar flavors and delicate texture. This is wonderful as is, but whipped cream enhances it beautifully.

MAKES 4–6 SERVINGS

1½ cups all-purpose flour

½ teaspoon salt

1 teaspoon baking powder

1 teaspoon baking soda

½ teaspoon freshly grated nutmeg

½ teaspoon ground ginger

1 teaspoon ground cinnamon

2 cups persimmon pulp (see Note)

2 cups buttermilk

½ cup (1 stick) unsalted butter, softened to room temperature

1½ cups sugar

3 large eggs

Heat the oven to 350°. Generously butter a 4 × 8 × 12-inch loaf pan. In a medium bowl, combine the flour, salt, baking powder, baking soda, nutmeg, ginger, and cinnamon. Use a fork or a whisk to stir them together and combine them evenly and well. In another bowl, combine the persimmon pulp and buttermilk and stir with a large spoon or a whisk to mix them evenly and well.

In a large bowl, combine the butter and sugar. Use an electric mixer, a large spoon, or a whisk to beat them until they are creamy and well-combined. Add the eggs, one at a time, beating well after each addition. Add the persimmon mixture and beat by hand using a spoon or a whisk until the mixture is smoothly and evenly combined.

Add the flour mixture and stir well, scraping the bowl to mix everything together into a smooth, thick batter. Pour the batter into the prepared pan and bake at 350° for 1–1¼ hours, or until the pudding has risen nicely and become firm but not dry. Transfer to a cooling rack or a folded kitchen towel and let stand for several minutes before serving. Serve hot, warm, or at room temperature.

NOTE ❋ You will need about 1 quart (3–4 cups) of ripe persimmons, to yield 2 cups of persimmon pulp.

From *Bill Neal's Southern Cooking: Revised and Enlarged Edition* by Bill Neal. Copyright © 1989 by William Franklin Neal. Used by permission of the publisher. www.uncpress.unc.edu

Persimmon Cookies

These chewy, nut- and raisin-studded gems are like little cakes, bursting with the rich, autumnal flavor of persimmons, but offering the easy portable pleasures of a cookie. Their flavor deepens on the second day, so try not to eat them all up before they have time to show off that enhancement!

MAKES ABOUT 3 DOZEN COOKIES

2 cups all-purpose flour
1 teaspoon ground cinnamon
½ teaspoon ground ginger
½ teaspoon ground cloves
½ teaspoon salt
1 cup chopped walnuts or pecans
1 cup raisins
1 cup sugar
½ cup (1 stick) butter, softened
1 large egg
1 cup persimmon purée
1 teaspoon baking soda

Heat the oven to 350°. Generously grease a baking sheet or line it with parchment paper. In a medium bowl, combine the flour, cinnamon, ginger, cloves, and salt. Use a whisk or a fork to stir them together evenly and well. Add the walnuts or pecans and the raisins and stir to mix them into the flour.

In a large bowl, combine the butter and the sugar and use an electric mixer to beat them together well. When they are soft and completely combined, add the egg and beat until the mixture is soft, fluffy, and smoothly combined. Add the persimmon purée and the baking soda and beat well.

Add the flour mixture to the butter mixture and stir gently with a wooden spoon or a spatula to mix everything together just until the flour disappears. The batter will be very thick.

Scoop the dough into rounded 2-inch portions and place them on the prepared baking sheet about 2 inches apart. Bake at 350° for 10–12 minutes, or until the cookies have risen and are plump, shiny, and nicely browned. Remove to a cooling rack or a large platter and let cool to room temperature. Store in an airtight container for up to 5 days.

Bill Smith's Persimmon Pound Cake

My friend Bill Smith loves the old-time pleasures of classic recipes, but he never gets stuck in the food museum, worshipping the past. His sense of culinary possibilities delights the regulars at Crook's Corner in Chapel Hill, North Carolina, from his famous cheese pork and spicy green Tabasco chicken to chestnut pudding and his springtime inspiration, honeysuckle sorbet. He serves tons of traditional persimmon pudding during the fall and winter but keeps his menu interesting by playing with nontraditional ways to enjoy the wild fruit. I adore his persimmon pound cake, which bakes up with a sweet, toothsome crust and a dense, moist crumb.

MAKES ONE 10-INCH CAKE

3¼ cups all-purpose flour

2 teaspoons baking powder

1 teaspoon ground cinnamon

½ teaspoon grated nutmeg

½ teaspoon ground ginger

½ teaspoon baking soda

½ teaspoon salt

½ cup buttermilk

1 teaspoon pure vanilla extract

1 cup (2 sticks) butter, softened

1 cup sugar

1 cup light brown sugar, lightly packed

4 large eggs

1 cup persimmon purée

Heat the oven to 350°. Generously grease a 10-inch tube pan or Bundt pan, using butter, shortening, or vegetable oil.

In a medium bowl, combine the flour, baking powder, cinnamon, nutmeg, ginger, baking soda, and salt. Using a whisk or a fork, stir to mix everything together evenly and well. Combine the buttermilk and vanilla in a small bowl and stir well.

Using an electric mixer, beat the butter at medium speed until light and fluffy. Add the sugars and beat at high speed, stopping often to scrape the bowl, to combine the ingredients evenly and well. Add the eggs, one at a time, beating well after each addition. Add the persimmon purée and beat at low speed to incorporate it into the butter mixture.

Add half the flour mixture to the persimmon batter and use a large spoon or whisk to incorporate the flour just until it disappears into the batter. Add half the buttermilk and stir well. Repeat with the remaining flour and buttermilk, stirring and scraping gently, just enough to bring everything together into a smooth, evenly combined batter. Don't overmix.

Scrape the batter into the prepared pan and bake at 350° for 50–60 minutes, or until the cake rises, becomes firm and dry, and just begins to pull away from the sides of the pan. The cake should feel springy to the touch, and a knife blade or skewer inserted into the center of the cake should come out clean.

Place the cake on a wire cooling rack or a folded kitchen towel and let cool to room temperature. Serve accompanied if you wish by vanilla ice cream or whipped cream.

Adrienne Carpenter's Persimmon Cheesecake

Adrienne Carpenter delights customers at the weekly farmers' market in Winston-Salem, North Carolina, with good things from her Sweet Petunia Bakery. Her biscotti, sticky buns, gingersnaps, and seasonal cobblers disappear fast, as does her extraordinary persimmon cheesecake, a seasonal treat that won my heart. She came up with it as a way to make good use of the abundance of wild persimmons she gathers each fall. This is best if chilled overnight, so plan to make it at least a day in advance if possible. Since this makes a very large cheesecake, perfect for a holiday gathering or big celebration, you'll be glad to know that it can even be made two to three days ahead. Keep it refrigerated until an hour or two before serving time.

MAKES 10–12 SERVINGS

FOR THE CRUST

3 cups finely chopped pecans
1 cup graham cracker or gingersnap cookie crumbs
1/2 cup light or dark brown sugar, lightly packed
4 tablespoons unsalted butter, melted

FOR THE FILLING

2 cups persimmon purée
3 (8-ounce) packages cream cheese, at room temperature
1 1/4 cups sugar
3/4 cup sour cream
1/2 teaspoon ground cinnamon
1/2 teaspoon ground ginger
8 large eggs

1¾ cups sour cream

3 tablespoons sugar

2 tablespoons Amaretto liqueur or 2 teaspoons
   almond extract

Heat the oven to 325°. Generously grease a 10-inch springform pan using butter, shortening, vegetable oil, or nonstick baking spray.

To make the crust, in a large bowl, combine the pecans, brown sugar, and crumbs. Use a fork or a whisk to mix them evenly and well. Add the butter and stir until the mixture is evenly combined. Using your hands or a small, flat-bottomed saucepan press the mixture into the bottom and 1 inch up the sides of the prepared pan. Bake at 325° for 12 minutes. Remove and set aside on a cooling rack or a folded kitchen towel to cool completely.

To make the filling, combine the persimmon purée and cream cheese in the bowl of a food processor and pulse a few times. Add the sugar, sour cream, cinnamon, and ginger and turn the processor on. Drop the eggs, one at a time, into the feeding shoot and process until smooth. You may need to scrape down the sides of the bowl occasionally.

Pour the filling into the cooled crust. Bake until the cheese-cake is fairly firm and mostly set, 1–1½ hours; the center will be a little jiggly.

Meanwhile, prepare the topping. In a medium bowl, combine the sour cream, sugar, and Amaretto or almond extract. Stir well, using a whisk or a fork, until the mixture is smooth. Cover and refrigerate while the cheesecake bakes.

When the cheesecake is done, remove it from the oven. Spread the topping over the warm cheesecake, leaving a 1-inch border around the edges. Return to the oven and bake for 10 minutes more.

Remove the cheesecake from oven and place it on a cooling rack or a folded kitchen towel. Let it cool completely. Cover loosely with foil or plastic wrap and refrigerate for at least 3 hours or overnight. To serve, remove the outer ring of the pan and place the cheesecake on a serving plate or cake stand. Serve cold, cool, or at room temperature.

NOTE ✱ This recipe calls for a food processor with a 10- to 12-cup capacity. If the machine seems too full, remove some of the filling and process it in batches, stirring everything back together after it has been processed. Or use a handheld mixer or a whisk to combine everything well.

Quince

The more I learn about the ancient pome fruit known as quince, the more I wonder why it is not a star among the fruits grown and loved here in the South. Why don't we don't see quince trees blooming in parks, around town, standing sentinel over community gardens, and decorating the countryside? Its charms are many, both as an ornamental tree and as a cherished food.

Quince has its very own genus, *Cydonia*, and the mellifluous species name, *Cydonia oblongata*. Native to Iran and Azerbaijan, this ancient tree's leaves are large, soft, and deep green, and its sizable bowl-shaped flowers bloom white with delicate pink accents. It grows to a manageable fifteen feet, making harvesting easy, and needs little pruning or fuss. It thrives in cooler climates and is self-pollinating—you need only one quince tree to grow the wonderful fruit. Quinces can be picked green and allowed to ripen in a bowl on the kitchen counter, providing a marvelous perfume that fills the house.

Even the infinite depictions of quince fruit, flowers, and trees in works of art from antiquity through the modern era testify to its charm. Scholars believe that the fruit described in Greek mythology as the golden apples of the Hesperides and as the favorite of Aphrodite, the goddess of love, are actually quinces. And in the early cookbook written by the Roman writer Apicius in the fifth century CE you'll find recipes for quinces stewed with honey and cooked with leeks.

For cooks, there's even more magic. Since colonial times, recipe writers have suggested poaching quinces in simple syrup, cooking them into jam and jelly, using them to flavor spirited beverages such as cordials and ratafia, and baking them into pies and tarts. Quinces are lovely combined with apples and pears as an enhancement to their flavor, and their prodigious amount of pectin makes them a valued ingredient in preserves and jams. There's even the magical property of color transformation. Raw quinces change from white to rosy pink and even a rustic red over time as they cook into jam.

Fragrant, beautiful, delicious, and a gardener's delight, quince is a glorious, delicious, and useful fruit, so why don't we don't see more quince trees in our midst? I say it's the challenge to the cook. Put frankly, quinces are troublesome. Their flesh is quite hard, and they're difficult to peel and core. Once peeled, they oxidize extremely quickly and turn brown if they aren't held in acidulated water. Worst of all, they are inedible raw, so turning this fruit into food involves a multistep process. While a few varieties are said to be acceptable and even tasty in their uncooked state, those are not the ones that historically have been grown in the South. In addition, quinces are extremely susceptible to the insidious fire blight disease, which spreads quickly from tree to tree. A quince tree in an orchard exposes other trees to this destructive disease, adding to quince's fall from favor in the twentieth-century South.

Despite these disincentives and complications, the movement back toward local, sustainable, seasonal, and flavorful food makes quinces worthy of appreciation. In the last few years, farmers' markets have begun to feature the lumpy, curvaceous fall fruit, and even supermarket produce sections here in North Carolina occasionally carry quinces for brief periods of time. *Membrillio*, the fantastically delicious deep-peach-colored fruit paste, has found favor among food lovers recently, especially in its classic pairing with manchego cheese, a dish known as Romeo y Julieta. So they take a little time and trouble—so what? Let's join the Slow Food people who have added a quince variety to the Ark of Taste. The quince is lovable, worth the time it takes to prepare it, and abundantly generous in the gifts it gives back, as a tree and as a pleasure of the table.

Quince Compote

Compote: A demure and lovely name for a simple, pleasing bowl of sweetened stewed fruit. Capturing the distinct flavor and rosy hue of cooked quince, this recipe transforms the knobby, fuzzy, and difficult-to-peel fruit into a dear little dessert. Most recipes call for peeling quinces before poaching them in this way. In her recipe for quince compote in The Taste of Country Cooking, *Edna Lewis calls for unpeeled quince, so that's what I use. Either way is fine, so do what suits you. Handle whole quinces gently, as despite their sturdy-looking appearance, they can easily be bruised. This compote cooks low and slow, no boiling required—or even allowed! Eat this within 5 days, and if you still have syrup left, think cocktails, ice cream, or fruit salad as places to use it up.*

MAKES 6–8 SERVINGS

3 pounds quinces
5–6 cups water
1 cup sugar
¼ cup honey

Gently wash the quinces and rub them with a clean, soft kitchen towel to remove any fuzz. Cut them lengthwise into quarters and cut away their cores, stems, and blossom ends. Combine the quinces, water, sugar, and honey in a large saucepan or Dutch oven. (There should be enough water in the pan to cover the fruit by 1 inch.) Bring to a gentle boil over medium-high heat, stirring well to dissolve the sugar and honey. Adjust the heat to maintain a gentle simmer, and cook until the quinces have softened nicely, 45–60 minutes. Be patient—it may take longer. Test for tenderness with the tip of a sharp knife or a fork.

When the quinces are tender, remove from heat and cool to room temperature. Transfer the poached fruit and syrup to a container, cover, and chill for up to 1 week. Serve warm, at room temperature, cool, or cold.

NOTE ❃ If you love this elegant treat, explore its possibilities with variations like these: As the quinces begin to simmer, stir in a few slices of fresh ginger a big sprig of mint, or a small sprig of fresh rosemary. You could also add a few allspice berries or cloves, a cinnamon stick, cardamom pods, or a star anise. Then there's orange or lemon peel cut into long strips, or slender threads from a zester, or a teaspoon of grated peel.

Dulce de Membrillo

Quince paste enjoys so much affection among European cooks but lacks a following here in the United States. To make quince paste, or what the Spanish call membrillo, *sturdy quinces are poached, mashed, and then slowly cooked down with sugar to an exquisitely flavorful and luminously colored paste. As it cooks down, the ivory-colored raw fruit turns pale orange, then dusky pink, and finally a handsome rust color. Lemon juice is typically added to brighten its flavor. Simply prepared, dulce de membrillo keeps well, and it delights as a snack, a candy, and an hors d'oeurve.*

The classic combination of membrillo and manchego, a sheep's-milk cheese produced in the La Mancha region of Spain, is known as Romeo y Julieta. It's also enjoyed with rich, crunchy marcona almonds and sherry or red wine.

MAKES ONE 9-INCH PAN OF QUINCE PASTE

2 pounds quinces

Water

2 cups sugar

2 tablespoons fresh lemon juice

Generously grease an 8-inch-square baking pan or two standard loaf pans with vegetable oil. Cut a piece of parchment paper large enough to fit the width of the pan and to extend at least 6 inches above the edges of the pan. Press the paper into the pan and oil it. (The parchment paper will enable you to lift the membrillo out of the pan easily when it is ready to enjoy.)

Gently wash the quinces and rub them with a clean, soft kitchen towel to remove any fuzz. Peel them, quarter them lengthwise, and cut away their cores, stems, and blossom ends. Chop them into large chunks and place them in a medium saucepan. Add enough water to cover the fruit by 1 inch and bring to a lively boil over medium-high heat. Adjust the heat to maintain a gentle but lively simmer and cook until the quinces have softened and become tender enough to be easily mashed with a fork, 25–30 minutes. Remove from the heat, drain well, and set aside to cool.

When the fruit is cool, add the sugar. Mash the fruit using a potato masher, and then press it through a fine-mesh sieve, scraping the rounded bottom of the sieve to capture all of the purée. Return the purée to the saucepan and continue cooking over medium heat, stirring often to prevent it from sticking to the pan or burning. Cook for 1–1½ hours, or until the quince has darkened to a rosy hue and is thicker than applesauce but not completely set. You should be able to pour it out in nice big plops and mound it up nicely.

When the paste is ready, spread it out evenly into the prepared pan and let it sit at room temperature overnight to firm up and dry out further. You should be able to cut it into squares that hold their shape. If it still seems too soft, bake it in the oven at 175° for about 1 hour.

When cool, firm, and dry, transfer the paste to a covered container and store in a cool place or in the refrigerator for up to 3 months. To serve, cut into small squares and enjoy as an appetizer or a snack or with cheeses and wine after a meal.

Nicole Taylor's Fried Quince Pies

This recipe presents a lovely reminder of the South's culinary past. Cookbook author and food journalist Nicole Taylor tucks an old-school ingredient, quince, into an old-school dish, fried pies, and the results are memorable. Fried pies were often made with dried fruit, particularly apples and peaches, allowing home cooks to bring summer and fall fruit's pleasures to the wintertime kitchen. Nicole cooks quinces gently with an array of sweet spices before encasing them in a homespun pastry made with buttermilk and lard. You can use butter or shortening or a combination of the two in place of lard here, and firm pears in place of quinces, keeping in mind that pears will become tender more quickly than their cousin.

MAKES ABOUT 12 PIES

FOR THE CRUST
4 cups all-purpose flour
1 teaspoon salt
1 cup very cold lard or butter
1 cup ice water
1/2 cup buttermilk

FOR THE FILLING
1/4 cup light brown sugar, packed
1/4 cup all-purpose flour
1/2 teaspoon ground cinnamon
1/4 teaspoon ground cardamom
1/4 teaspoon ground ginger
1/4 teaspoon ground nutmeg
1/4 teaspoon salt
1/4 teaspoon vanilla bean paste or pure vanilla extract

About 3 pounds quinces (to make 4 cups sliced),
    or firm pears
4 tablespoons butter
1 cup sugar
1½ cups lard or vegetable oil

To prepare the crust, using a fork, a whisk, or your hands, stir the flour and salt together in a large bowl. Add the lard to the flour, spooning up small lumps and scattering them around the bowl. (If using butter, cut it into ½-inch chunks before adding it to the flour.) Toss the flour gently with your hands to coat the lard, and, working quickly, mix, mash, and toss the mixture until crumbly bits with pea-sized chunks are formed. Add most of the water and the buttermilk and stir gently to form a dough. Turn the dough out onto a floured counter and gather it into a mound. Knead a few times, and then divide it into two portions. Wrap them each in plastic wrap, gently shaping them into disks, and refrigerate while you prepare the quince filling.

To make the filling, in a medium bowl, combine the brown sugar, flour, cinnamon, cardamom, ginger, nutmeg, salt, and vanilla bean paste or vanilla extract. Stir with a fork to mix everything evenly and well.

Gently wash the quinces and rub them with a clean, soft kitchen towel to remove any fuzz. Peel them, quarter them lengthwise, and cut away their cores, stems, and blossom ends. Chop the fruit into medium-sized pieces.

In a 12-inch skillet over medium heat, melt the butter and then add the brown sugar mixture and the quinces. Stir well and bring to a bubble. Adjust the heat to maintain the bubbling; cover and cook, stirring now and then, until the fruit is softened and juicy, about 15 minutes. Uncover, remove from heat and set aside to cool.

Roll out the chilled piecrust dough on a large, floured countertop, making it about ¼ inch thick. Using a 4-inch round cookie or biscuit cutter, cut the dough into circles (see Note). Spoon a generous tablespoon of quince filling onto each circle. Fold the dough over and use a fork to press the edges closed. Transfer the pies to a platter or a sheet pan and place them by the stove. Set out a platter lined with paper towels to hold the pies once they are cooked. Put the sugar in a shallow bowl.

In a large cast-iron skillet, heat the lard or vegetable oil over medium-high heat to 350°. Carefully add 3 or 4 pies to the hot oil; they should sizzle at once. Cook for 2–3 minutes, or until golden brown. Flip them over and cook on the other side until golden brown and cooked through, another 1–2 minutes. Carefully transfer them to the prepared platter or sheet pan. Repeat with the remaining pies. Roll the warm pies in the sugar to coat them nicely and set them on a cooling rack. Serve warm or at room temperature.

NOTE ❋ If you have a classic metal sifter as I do: its base is a great tool for cutting the pastry dough circles.

Moroccan-Inspired Lamb Stew with Quince

Aromatic and satisfying, this hearty dish pairs meat and fruit in a most inviting way. Flavors dance in the stewpot: sweet and savory spices, sharp lemon and luxurious honey, fresh parsley and earthy, robust lamb. Make this a day ahead of serving, and you will be rewarded with extra-deep and complex flavors; but know you will be challenged when it is done and ready and your game plan is to let it cool and reserve it for later! Discipline! Lamb shoulder is ideal for this dish, but any cut of lamb, or even beef, will work well. Use a heavy Dutch oven for this dish; if you have one made of cast iron or enameled cast iron, that would be an excellent choice here. This hearty stew goes wonderfully with couscous, rice, mashed potatoes, or lots of crusty bread.

MAKES 4 SERVINGS

2 teaspoons ground ginger

1 teaspoon ground cumin

1 teaspoon ground coriander

1 teaspoon ground cinnamon

1 teaspoon salt

1 teaspoon freshly ground black or white pepper

$1/2$ teaspoon cayenne pepper

3 tablespoons olive oil

$2^1/2$ pounds lamb shoulder or lamb stew meat,
    cut into 2-inch chunks

2 cups chopped onion

1 tablespoon chopped garlic

$3^1/2$ cups chicken broth or water

2 or 3 medium quinces (about $1^1/2$ pounds)

2 tablespoons honey

2 tablespoons fresh lemon juice

$1/2$ cup chopped cilantro or flat-leaf or curly parsley

In a small bowl, combine the ginger, cumin, coriander, cinnamon, salt, pepper, and cayenne. Use a fork to mix them together well, and set aside.

In a large, heavy Dutch oven, heat the oil over medium-high heat until a bit of onion added to it sizzles at once. Working in batches to avoid crowding the pan, scatter in about half the lamb, and let it cook undisturbed on one side until nicely browned, 1–2 minutes. Turn the lamb pieces and cook until the other side browns, 1–2 minutes more. Transfer the meat to a large bowl and continue until you've browned all the meat.

Add the onions to the pan and stir to mix them in with the oil. Cook until fragrant, about 1 minute. Stir in the garlic, and when you can catch its aroma in the pan, add the spice mixture and toss to mix everything well. Cook, tossing and stirring often, until the onions are shiny and tender and the spices are fragrant, 2–3 minutes more.

Return the meat to the pot, along with all juices in the bowl, and toss to mix everything evenly. Increase the heat to high, add the chicken broth, and bring to a lively boil. Stir well, reduce the heat to maintain an active but gentle simmer, and cook, stirring now and then, until the meat is tender and the sauce has thickened and developed a spiced, hearty flavor, 45–55 minutes.

Meanwhile, prepare the quinces. Gently wash them and rub them with a clean, soft kitchen towel to remove any fuzz. Peel them, halve them lengthwise, and cut away their cores, stems, and blossom ends. Cut each half lengthwise into 3 pieces and set aside.

When the lamb is tender, add the quinces to the Dutch oven and stir well. Cook, stirring occasionally, until the quince is fork-tender, about 30 minutes more. Add the honey, lemon juice, and cilantro or parsley, and stir well. Serve hot or warm.

Quince Ratafia

Sweet and boozy, ratafias are made by infusing a spirit such as brandy, corn whiskey, or wine with ripe fruit and sugar. A popular eighteenth-century tipple, this liqueur was popular in colonial American parlors and public houses. With their foundation an already distilled or fermented alcoholic beverage, ratafias were easily made at home by adding an array of flavorful goodies, from fruits, nuts, and herbs to berries, blossoms, and spices. This simple, elegant recipe is based on one by the extraordinary and eloquent English food writer Jane Grigson.

MAKES ABOUT 3 ½ CUPS

2 large, ripe quinces
1 cup sugar, plus more if needed
¼ teaspoon ground cinnamon
¼ teaspoon ground ginger
¼ teaspoon ground mace
Brandy or vodka

Sterilized a 1-quart jar with a tight-fitting lid as described on page 26.

Gently wash the quinces and wipe them carefully with a clean kitchen towel to remove any fuzz. Grate each quince in its entirety (the peel, core, and fruit) into a large bowl. Set aside.

Pour the sugar into the prepared jar. If it doesn't fill about ⅓ of the jar, add more. Add the cinnamon, ginger, and mace and stir with a fork to mix them well. Add the grated quince to the jar. Pour in enough brandy or vodka to fill the jar to within ½ inch of the top. Cover and seal it with the lid. Set aside for 2–3 months.

To serve, place a large fine-mesh strainer over a large bowl. Pour the contents of the jar into the strainer. Discard the contents of the strainer, and return the strained liquid to the jar. Cover and store at room temperature.

RATAFIA

The word "ratafia" refers to two different kinds of alcoholic beverages and a sweet cookie. In addition to the fruit-based liqueur featured in the Quince Ratafia recipe, a second type of drinkable ratafia is a fortified wine, in which marc brandy and unfermented grape juice are combined into a strong, sweet, potent drink. This second type of ratafia, usually commercially produced, remains a treasured spirit, particularly in France. The third type of ratafia is a simple cookie, made from finely ground almonds and egg whites, much like a classic macaroon.

Strawberries

Strawberries strike me as fancy and modern, cute cartoon creations, with that shiny crimson exterior under perfectly centered frilly green caps. In fact, they are a wild food treasure, with worldwide reach. This prolific perennial's roots reach back to prehistoric times, and it was lauded as both treat and medicine in ancient Rome. Ubiquitous commercially—grown in vast fields and shipped hither and yon—strawberries strike me as all-American fruits, not heirloom originals within southern food history.

Strawberries are indeed southern, valued long before colonial times. While they grow wild all over the Americas, strawberries are indigenous to the area settled by American colonists, from Massachusetts down to Florida. These heart-shaped, conspicuous berries were revered and enjoyed by Indigenous peoples, including members of the Cherokee nation, who held *Fragara virginiana* in great esteem. They celebrated strawberries as the herald of springtime, and because they understood the tiny red berries' medicinal value, they sought them out during the fruits' fleeting season to use for healing, as well as for nourishment. Along with pawpaws in late summer and wild persimmons in the fall, wild strawberries offered sustenance and delight in season, year in and year out.

The desire to extend strawberries' brief season led to efforts to domestication them. French horticulturists were working to cultivate strawberries by the fourteenth century, bringing wild woodland berries into the garden and experimenting with crossing species. In 1380 CE, France's King Charles V's royal gardens contained 1,200 strawberry plants, and by the sixteenth century, domestication efforts were finding success in England as well as on the European continent and in South America. Artists have celebrated the tiny, wild springtime beauties over centuries, featuring strawberries in paintings, miniatures, and illuminated manuscripts.

Today's garden strawberry, *Fragaria ananassa*, resulted from the hybridization efforts of horticulturists in mid-eighteenth century France. Scientists there combined two woodland berries, *Fragara virginiana*, from North America, and *Fragaria chiloensis*, a large, sturdy strawberry domesticated by the Mapuche and Huilliche people in what is now Chile. When transported to northern France and crossed with the tiny, sweet, and fragrant *F. virginiana*, a new species, *F. x ananassa* came into being. This is the modern garden strawberry, which is grown commercially and in home gardens around the world today.

Early cookbooks and southern gardening records include references to strawberries but mostly the wild fruit brought in to early colonial gardens or simply gathered in the woods and fields during their brief season. Thomas Jefferson delighted in sharing berries and plants and seeking new cultivars, but his strawberries were a brief pleasure.

For new gardeners seeking to bring southern fruits into their repertoire, strawberries make great sense. They require only a small area for cultivation; they produce abundantly within a year or two of planting; they thrive throughout most of the South; they require no trellises, stakes, arbors, or pruning; and they don't have thorns.

Just as strawberries are easy and rewarding to grow, they offer cooks an abundance of wonderful ways to enjoy them, in addition to the pure pleasure of eating them by the bowlful, sprinkled with sugar and dolloped with clouds of whipped cream. Jam is the place to start. Strawberry freezer jam recipes make basic preserving easy Toss them with just enough sugar to draw out a syrup, stir them into yogurt, tuck them into shortcakes, or mix them with spirits to make a cordial. Strawberries shine, whether you grow your own, pluck a pail's worth at a pick-your-own farm, or find them at southern farmers' markets in May and June.

Strawberry-Rhubarb Pie

If you want visible and edible proof that winter is going, going, gone, this pie is your ticket. A southern springtime classic, strawberry-rhubarb pie combines two distinctly different harbingers of spring—firm squared rhubarb pieces with round red-ripe summery berries—resulting in one glorious and gorgeous pie. It's simple to make, simply beautiful, and simply delicious. You can even use frozen rhubarb and frozen strawberries here straight from the freezer, no thawing required. Ice cream is optional here, but with a pink, juicy pie like this, it's never wrong.

MAKES ONE 9-INCH PIE

Pastry for a 9-inch double-crust pie (page 38)

1¼ cups sugar

¼ cup all-purpose flour or cornstarch

¼ teaspoon ground cinnamon

¼ teaspoon salt

3 cups chopped fresh rhubarb, cut into ½-inch chunks (about 1 pound)

2 pounds fresh strawberries, hulled and cut into 1-inch chunks (about 6 cups) (see Note)

1 tablespoon fresh lemon juice

2 tablespoons cold butter, cut into ¼-inch pieces

Heat the oven to 425°. Line a 9-inch pie pan with one of the rolled-out piecrusts, letting the pastry extend 1 inch over the rim of the pie pan. In a large bowl, combine the sugar, flour or cornstarch, cinnamon, and salt and use a fork or a whisk to stir them together well. Add the rhubarb, strawberries, and lemon juice and use a large spoon to mix everything gently and well.

Transfer the fruit mixture to the piecrust and scatter the bits of cold butter evenly over the filling. Carefully drape the second rolled-out piecrust over the filling, and trim it so that it is even with the bottom crust. Fold the edges of the bottom crust up and around the top crust edges, and press to seal them together well. Use the back of a fork to press the edges together thoroughly, or pinch the crust into a handsome zigzag pattern all around the pie. Use a sharp knife to cut several slits in the top crust so that steam and juices can escape as the pie bakes.

Place the pie on a baking sheet lined with parchment paper or aluminum foil (which will catch any bubbling red syrup toward the end of baking time). Bake at 425° for 20 minutes, then lower the temperature to 350°. Continue baking until the pink filling bubbles up and the pastry is golden brown, 45–50 minutes more. Place the pie on a cooling rack or a folded kitchen towel and let it cool for at least 15 minutes. Serve warm or at room temperature.

NOTE ✳ You can use whole frozen strawberries for this pie; there is no need to thaw or chop them. You can also use frozen rhubarb, which comes chopped into 1-inch chunks. Add it frozen; no need to thaw it first.

Debbie Gooch's
Fresh Strawberry Bread

This recipe makes an irresistible and delicious quick bread that you will love. You can stir it together in just a few minutes, and enjoy it for several days, since keeps so well. You get two fragrant loaves from this recipe—one for now and one to freeze, or one for you and one for friends. Fresh strawberries are lovely, but frozen strawberries work wonderfully, too. Walnuts work nicely in place of pecans. Debbie picks strawberries during their season here in North Carolina each May and freezes them in 2-cup portions, sprinkled with a little sugar. That way she can make her irresistible strawberry bread all through the year.

MAKES TWO 9 × 5-INCH LOAVES

- 2 cups whole strawberries
- 3 cups all-purpose flour
- 2 cups plus 1 tablespoon sugar
- 1 tablespoon ground cinnamon
- 1 teaspoon salt
- 1 teaspoon baking soda
- 1¼ cups chopped pecans or walnuts
- 1¼ cups vegetable oil
- 4 large eggs, beaten well

Heat the oven to 350°. Coarsely chop the strawberries and place them in a large bowl. Sprinkle them with 1 tablespoon of the sugar and set aside. Generously butter two 9 × 5-inch loaf pans.

In a medium bowl, combine the flour, the remaining sugar, the cinnamon, the salt, and the baking soda. Use a whisk or a fork to mix them together well. Add the pecans or walnuts and toss to coat them with flour.

Stir the strawberries and then add the oil and eggs. Stir to combine everything evenly. Add the flour mixture to the strawberries and stir just until the flour is incorporated. Quickly divide the batter between the prepared pans. Bake at 350° for 45–50 minutes, or until the loaves have risen and browned nicely and a toothpick inserted in the center of the loaves comes out clean.

Set the loaves on a cooling rack or folded kitchen towels to cool to room temperature before turning them out of the pans.

Strawberry Coulis

Coulis is a simple sauce that showcases the jewel color and pure flavor of strawberries, which makes it wonderful accompaniment for a simple piece of pound cake, a bowl of ice cream, or a chic slice of lemon tart. But don't save it for dessert—imagine your bowl of morning oatmeal or yogurt elevated to a heavenly level by a crimson burst of pure strawberry goodness. You will want to always have this on hand, and it's easy to do so with its simple preparation. It keeps nicely for up to a week.

MAKES 3 ½ CUPS

3 cups fresh or frozen strawberries
⅓ cup sugar
1 tablespoon fresh lemon juice or lime juice

Trim and hull the strawberries and chop them coarsely. Combine the strawberries, sugar, and lemon juice in a medium saucepan. Bring to a lively boil and then adjust the heat to maintain a gentle simmer. Cook for 5 minutes, stirring now and then to dissolve the sugar.

Remove from the heat and use a potato masher to crush the berries to a coarse purée. Place a fine-mesh strainer over a medium bowl, and use the back of a spoon to press the strawberry juice through it. Discard the contents of the strainer and transfer the strawberry sauce to a jar. Cool to room temperature, cover, and refrigerate until needed.

Strawberry Shrub

Shrubs are a lovely means of preserving summertime berry goodness for sipping on the porch while lightning bugs flicker or by the fireplace come winter. Vinegar adds a tangy kick to the ruby fruit, making a syrup that can be added to club soda or sparkling water to make a homemade soft drink, or stirred into champagne, white wine, or a cocktail for a spirited refreshment.

MAKES ABOUT 3 CUPS

3 cups apple cider vinegar
3 cups trimmed and quartered fresh or frozen strawberries
3 cups sugar

Prepare a large glass jar with a tight-fitting lid as directed on page 26.

In a medium saucepan, heat the vinegar until it is just about to break into a bubbling boil and remove it from the heat. Place the strawberries in the prepared jar and pour the vinegar over them, making sure they are covered by an inch of vinegar. Let cool to room temperature and then cover tightly. Set aside in a cool, dark place for 24–48 hours (be sure the jar is not exposed to heat or light).

Strain the vinegar into a medium saucepan and discard the solids. Add the sugar to the vinegar and bring to a rolling boil, stirring to dissolve the sugar. As soon as the sugar is dissolved, remove the pan from the heat and let the shrub cool to room temperature. Pour the shrub into a clean, sterilized jar and cover tightly. Store in the refrigerator for up to 6 months.

Watermelon

If you grew up in the South back when phones were known as "telephones" and anchored to the wall, before they took pictures, you might be aware of the fact that watermelons were at one time both a highlight and a delight of summer. Encased in bright-green torpedo-shaped, biodegradable containers and amply studded with sturdy little seeds, they were considered to be worth the space and mess required to enjoy their many pleasures. All that was before the modern agricultural miracle made them ubiquitous, polyseasonal, cheap, petite, and almost devoid of seeds.

Sometime in the second half of the twentieth century, Americans' longtime devotion to convenience and availability caught the attention of food-tech people, who figured out how to engineer a sterile watermelon—a smaller, seedless version with a sturdier shell and a thinner rind. So, now that watermelons are available to us year-round in the produce section of supermarkets nationwide, we seldom look to the watermelon as a sweet, juicy cure for the summertime blues. With air-conditioning a thing, and entertainment aplenty via smartphones, seed-spitting contests hold little excitement.

What would King Tutankhamun think if he could see a twenty-first-century watermelon? We know his people placed watermelon seeds in his tomb, suggesting that *Citrullus lanatus* was a cherished item. Was it as a royal snack or a crop to plant once he had journeyed across the River Styx? While most sources agree that watermelons originated on the African continent, they don't concur on the specific location. In addition, disputes remain over whether the sweet, juicy red watermelon beloved throughout the modern world is related to the small, round, dry-fleshed citron melon, *Citrullus caffer*, which is indigenous to the Kalahari Desert in the southwestern region of the continent.

We know that watermelons were cultivated widely in the Nile Valley from the second millennium BCE, and that by the tenth century CE they were grown in China and India. By 1158 CE they were growing in Seville, and soon afterward in Europe as far north as the heat-loving vines could thrive. By the 1600s, watermelons were commonplace in European gardens and in America after Spanish explorers planted them in St. Augustine, Florida, around 1575 CE. Native Americans took watermelon cultivation farther into Florida and northward and westward as far as the Mississippi River. Recipes for watermelon-rind pickles began to appear in recipe collections beginning in the early 1800s, a reminder of this fruit's most unique property: it's 100 percent edible—flesh, seeds, and even its rind.

What's in a name? Despite its name, the watermelon belongs to the gourd family, *Cucurbitaceae*, and is related to cucumbers and winter melon rather than to muskmelons such as cantaloupe and honeydew and the French charentais and cavaillon melons. If you're looking for old-school watermelons that are ideal for making watermelon rind preserves and pickles, check out garden seed suppliers, where the Tom Watson, Georgia Rattlesnake, and Black Diamond cultivars might still be found.

Commercial priorities in the 1880s led to breeding for "rhino-hided" or boxcar watermelons, which have rinds thick enough to allow the fruit to be stacked layers high in boxcars for distribution. Disease resistance was also a major consideration, along with consumers' desire for smaller, seedless cultivars with thinner rinds. One legendary cultivar, the Bradford watermelon, was a fruit-world superstar from 1840 through the 1920s, but its superb sweetness and flavor eventually ceased to find favor in the mass-production-oriented twentieth-century marketplace.

Thankfully, the Bradford family has been growing and preserving these heirloom beauties on their own South Carolina farms for generations. Because of their dedication, as well as the tenacity and enthusiasm of people like David Shields and Glenn Roberts of the Carolina Gold Rice Foundation and members of the Slow Food movement, including it in the Ark of Taste, the Bradford watermelon is making a comeback.

Watermelon-Rind Pickles

This traditional southern relish shows the creativity and optimism of old-time cooks who considered the rinds of watermelons a source of culinary pleasure. Made from the green-tinted outer layer of the beloved summertime treat, these sweet, tender pickles have a slightly tangy kick and a very delicate note of cucumber. The cucumber connection makes sense given that both cucumbers and watermelons belong to the botanical family Cucurbitaceae. *During my childhood these translucent, golden-tinged pickles appeared regularly in a small cut-glass dish at Sunday dinner, and they grace the center of a deviled egg plate at my family reunion each June. Plan ahead when making these pickles, as the process begins with a 5-hour soak in salted water. You can sterilize the jars while the pickles are cooking in the sweet-and-sour brine. (page 26)*

MAKES ABOUT 4 CUPS
(2 PINT OR 4 HALF-PINT JARS)

---

1 small watermelon (about 5 pounds)

2 quarts water

$\frac{1}{3}$ cup salt

3 cups sugar

$1\frac{1}{2}$ cups white vinegar or apple cider vinegar

$1\frac{1}{2}$ cups water

Quarter the watermelon lengthwise. Cut each quarter into triangular slices about 1 inch thick. Cut away and reserve the pulp, leaving the white rind. Using a sturdy vegetable peeler or a sharp knife, pare away the green skin on the outside of the rind. Cut the rind into 1- by 2-inch pieces. You will have about 4 cups. In a medium bowl, combine the water and the salt. Stir well to dissolve the salt and then add the watermelon rind to the bowl. Set aside for 5 hours.

Drain the watermelon rind and rinse it well. Transfer it to a medium saucepan and add fresh water to cover it completely. Bring to a rolling boil over high heat and then reduce the heat to maintain a gentle boil. Cook until the rind softens and takes on a slightly golden hue, 10–15 minutes. Drain well and set aside.

In the same saucepan, combine the sugar, vinegar, and water to a rolling boil, stirring to dissolve the sugar and form a thin syrup. Add the watermelon rind to the syrup, and let it return to a boil. Adjust the heat to maintain a gentle simmer and cook, stirring occasionally, until the rind is tender, translucent, and golden, with a pleasing tangy taste, about 1 hour.

Scoop the pickles out of the brine and divide them among the prepared jars. Carefully divide the hot syrup among the jars, allowing ½ inch of space between the syrup and the top of the jar. (Discard any remaining syrup or use it to make a salad dressing). Let cool to room temperature, and then cover each jar tightly. Store in the refrigerator for up to 3 weeks.

Kathy Strahs's
Watermelon-Lime Jelly Cubes

Wiggly-jiggly, ruby-red, and wonderful, these watermelon delights from my friend Kathy Strahs generate smiles and not just from youngsters. I love having a container of these geometric treats in the refrigerator so that when I want a snack or need an accent to a busy-day lunch, all I need to do is reach for some cool cubes. For cookouts and picnics, these scarlet squares are a cool, make-ahead addition to the menu, as an appetizer or among the sweets.

MAKES 64 CUBES

8–10 cups cubed, seedless watermelon

¾ cup sugar

5 (¼-ounce) packets unflavored gelatin

3 tablespoons fresh lime juice or lemon juice

⅓ cup chopped fresh mint (optional)

Grease an 8 × 8-inch glass or ceramic baking dish or metal baking pan with vegetable oil, and wipe out any excess with a paper towel. Purée the watermelon in a food processor or blender, working in batches if necessary. Pour the purée through a fine-mesh sieve into a medium bowl to strain out the pulp. You will need a total of 6 cups of strained watermelon juice.

Transfer 1 cup of the watermelon juice to a small saucepan. Add the sugar and stir well. Bring to a boil over medium-high heat, stirring until the sugar dissolves completely. Remove from the heat and set aside.

Measure out a second cup of the watermelon juice to a large bowl and sprinkle the gelatin over the surface. Stir to mix it into the watermelon juice and then let stand for 1 minute.

Pour the hot watermelon juice / sugar mixture into the bowl. Stir well with a whisk or a large spoon to dissolve the gelatin completely and mix everything well. Add the remaining watermelon juice to the bowl along with the lime or lemon juice. Stir to combine everything well.

Pour the gelatin mixture into the prepared dish or pan. Use a spoon to skim off and discard any foam that may have formed on the surface. Refrigerate the gelatin for at least 4 hours, or until it is completely firm and set. Cut the gelatin into 1-inch cubes and garnish each cube with mint. Serve chilled.

NOTE ✳ If you are using a blender to purée the watermelon, you may need to add a little water in order to move the blades. You can also add some of the strained juice from the first batches back into the blender to coax the fruit along in its transformation from solid to liquid.

From *The 8x8 Cookbook: Square Meals for Weeknight Family Dinners, Desserts and More—in One Perfect 8x8-Inch Dish*, by Kathy Strahs. Copyright © 2015 by Kathy Lipscomb Strahs. Burnt Cheese Press, 2015.

Thai-Inspired
Watermelon-Pineapple Salad

Growing up in North Carolina, I learned to live with the sultry, penetrating heat of summertime. Living in Thailand as a Peace Corps volunteer, I found the blistering heat familiar but still a challenge. One brilliant culinary tradition eased the burden: the simple dessert course of watermelon and pineapple, arranged in big slices on a platter and inundated with shaved ice. Sweet, juicy, bright in color and flavor, the two fruits were a magic respite from the hottest afternoon's heat. I love combining the two fruits in a bowl with fresh mint and little honey. Even inside with air conditioning's cushion, this simple dish brings cool pleasure every time.

MAKES 4 SERVINGS

---

3 tablespoons fresh lime juice or lemon juice

2 tablespoons honey

3 cups watermelon chunks

3 cups sliced pineapple, cut in bite-sized triangles

¼ cup thinly sliced fresh mint

2 teaspoons dried red pepper flakes

In a large bowl, combine the lime or lemon juice and honey and stir with a whisk or a fork to combine them evenly and well. Add the watermelon, pineapple, mint, and red pepper flakes. Gently toss and stir to flavor the fruit and mix in the mint. Serve at once or chill for an hour or two and serve cold.

Acknowledgments

I have always loved to eat, and I've loved to cook as long as I can remember. What a gift to be able to work in the world of food, one that is overflowing with people so kind, generous, funny, creative, interesting, and inspiring that I never tire of looking to see who's cooking what, where, how, and why. The circle of friends-in-food who fill my life and work with meaning and joy is so big that I would need a book to list them all, but I want to thank one friend in particular: Jill O'Connor, whose listening ear, culinary and everyday smarts, and hilarious insights and commentary keep me going, laughing all the while.

For the privilege of working on this book, I am deeply grateful to my editor, Elaine Maisner, at the University of North Carolina Press, who created this excellent and worthy series of books celebrating southern food in such a detailed and illuminating way. It's an honor to join this distinguished circle of authors, and a joy to work on this volume, a subject fascinating and dear to me. I appreciate the excellent work of Mary Carley Caviness and Allison Shay in bringing this book from an idea to a real, readable, cookable book, and of Gina Mahalek in getting the good word out about *Fruit*. I am thankful to these good people for generously sharing their southern fruit recipes with me: Adrienne Carpenter, Martha Hall Foose, Debbie Gooch, Sandra Gutierrez, Jill Warren Lucas, Vimala Ramajendran, Bill Smith, Kathy Strahs, Nicole Taylor, and Sherri Brooks Vinton. Most of all, I am grateful to my wonderful family, especially my two beautiful, funny, and wise sisters, Linda and Susanne, and my fabulous, handsome, happy, brilliant and sweet husband, William Tsung Liang Lee, who loves my cooking, shows up hungry and happy for every meal, believes in me no matter what, and makes it all a feast.

For Further Reading

Albala, Ken, and Rosanna Nafziger. *The Lost Art of Real Cooking; Rediscovering the Pleasures of Traditional Food One Recipe at a Time.* New York: Perigee/The Penguin Group, 2010.

Anderson, Jean. *Jean Anderson's Preserving Guide: How to Pickle and Preserve, Can and Freeze, Dry and Store Vegetables and Fruits.* 1976. Chapel Hill: University of North Carolina Press, 2012.

Barrow, Cathy. *Mrs. Wheelbarrow's Practical Pantry: Recipes and Techniques for Year-Round Preserving.* New York: W. W. Norton, 2014.

Bennett, Chris. *Southeast Foraging: 120 Wild and Flavorful Edibles, from Angelica to Wild Plums.* Portland, Ore.: Timber Press, 2015.

Bir, Sara. *The Pocket Pawpaw Cookbook.* Marietta, Ohio: The Sausagetarian, 2015.

Boning, Charles R. *Florida's Best Fruiting Plants: Native and Exotic Trees, Shrubs, and Vines.* Sarasota, Fla.: Pineapple Press, 2006.

Castle, Sheri. *The New Southern Garden Cookbook: Enjoying the Best from Homegrown Gardens, Farmers' Markets, Roadside Stands, & CSA Farm Boxes.* Chapel Hill: University of North Carolina Press, 2011.

Cheuk, Beth L. *Thomas Jefferson's Monticello.* The Thomas Jefferson Foundation, Inc., 2002.

Crump, Nancy Carter. *Hearthside Cooking: Early American Southern Cuisine Updated for Today's Hearth and Cookstove.* Chapel Hill: University of North Carolina Press, 2008.

Davidson, Alan. *Fruit: A Connoisseur's Guide and Cookbook.* New York: Simon & Schuster, 1991.

Diacono, Mark. *Fruit: River Cottage Handbook No. 9.* London: Bloomsbury, 2011.

Fisher, Abby. *What Mrs. Fisher Knows about Old Southern Cooking: Soups, Preserves, Pickles, Etc.* San Francisco: Women's Co-Operative Printing Office, 1881; reprint, Bedford, Mass.: Applewood Books, 1995.

Ghazarian, Barbara. *Simply Quince.* Pacific Grove, Calif.: Mayreni Publications, 2009.

Gollner, Adam Leith. *The Fruit Hunters: A Story of Nature, Adventure, Commerce and Obsession.* New York: Scribner, 2008.

Grigson, Jane. *Good Things*. New York: Atheneum, 1984; reprint, Lincoln, Neb.: University of Nebraska Press, 2006.

———. *Jane Grigson's Fruit Book*. New York: Atheneum, 1982.

Grovner, Yvonne J., Cornelia Walker Bailey, and Doc. Bill. *The Foods of Georgia's Barrier Islands: A Gourmet Food Guide of Native American, Geechee and European Influences on the Golden Isles*. Sapelo Island, Ga.: Grovner, Bailey, and Thomas Press, 2004.

Lewis, Edna. *In Pursuit of Flavor*. New York: Alfred A. Knopf, 1988

———. *The Taste of Country Cooking*. New York: Alfred A. Knopf, 1975.

Lewis, Edna, and Scott Peacock. *The Gift of Southern Cooking: Recipes and Revelations from Two Great American Cooks*. New York: Alfred A. Knopf, 2003.

Lundy, Ronni. *Butterbeans to Blackberries: Recipes from the Southern Garden*. New York: North Point Press, 1999.

McClellan, Marisa. *Food In Jars: Preserving in Small Batches Year-Round*. Philadelphia: Running Press, 2011.

Meech, William Witler. *Quince Culture: An Illustrated Handbook*. 1888. Bedford, Mass.: Applewood Books, 2009.

Moore, Andrew. *Pawpaw: In Search of America's Forgotten Fruit*. White River Junction, Vt.: Chelsea Green Publishing, 2015.

Page, Karen, and Andrew Dornenberg. *The Flavor Bible: The Essential Guide to Culinary Creativity, Based on the Wisdom of America's Most Imaginative Chefs*. New York: Little, Brown, 2008.

Parsons, Russ. *How to Pick a Peach: The Search for Flavor from Farm to Table*. New York: Houghton Mifflin, 2007.

Reich, Lee. *Uncommon Fruits for Every Garden*. Portland, Ore.: Timber Press, 2004.

Rule, Cheryl Sternman. *Ripe: A Fresh, Colorful Approach to Fruits and Vegetables*. Philadelphia: Running Press, 2011.

Schloss, Andrew. *Homemade Liqueurs and Infused Spirits: Innovative Flavor Combinations, plus Homemade Versions of Kahlua, Cointreau and Other Popular Liqueurs*. North Adams, Mass.: Storey Publishing, 2013.

Strahs, Kathy. *The 8 x 8 Cookbook: Square Meals for Weeknight Family Dinners, Desserts and More—in One Perfect 8 x 8-Inch Dish*. Los Gatos, Calif.: Burnt Cheese Press, 2015.

Tartan, Beth. *North Carolina and Old Salem Cookery*. 1955. Chapel Hill: University of North Carolina Press, 1992.

Taylor, Nicole A. *The Up South Cookbook: Chasing Dixie in a Brooklyn Kitchen.* New York: The Countryman Press, 2015.

Tipton-Martin, Toni. *The Jemima Code: Two Centuries of African American Cookbooks.* Austin: University of Texas Press, 2015.

Vinton, Sheri Brooks. *Put 'Em Up! A Comprehensive Home Preserving Guide for the Creative Cook from Drying and Freezing to Canning and Pickling.* North Adams, Mass.: Storey Publishing, 2010.

———. *Put 'Em Up! Fruit. A Preserving Guide and Cookbook.* North Adams, Mass.: Storey Publishing, 2013.

Waters, Alice. *Chez Panisse Fruit.* New York: Harper Collins, 2002.

Weigl, Andrea. *Pickles & Preserves: A Savor the South Cookbook.* Chapel Hill: University of North Carolina Press, 2014.

West, Kevin. *Saving the Season: A Cook's Guide to Home Canning, Pickling, and Preserving.* New York: Alfred A. Knopf, 2013.

Index